Volume 39 Number 3 October 2015

Contents

Glossary

Glossary of terms 195

Editorial

The invisible disability 197
Mary Mather

Articles

Prenatal exposure to alcohol causes enduring brain damage 201
WA Phillips

Knowledge and opinions of professional groups concerning FASD in the UK 212
Raja Mukherjee, Elizabeth Wray, Leopold Curfs and Sheila Hollins

Identifying children who are at risk of FASD in Peterborough: working in a community clinic without access to gold standard diagnosis 225
Geraldine Gregory, Venkat Reddy and Clare Young

'I know that I'm in my own world; it's OK, they know me here': the challenge of coping with FASD in educational settings 235
Brian Roberts

The challenges of caring for a child with FASD 247
Julia Brown

Progress in addressing FASD in Scotland 256
Margaret Watts

Legal notes

England and Wales 263

Northern Ireland 266

Health notes

The problems of making a diagnosis of FAS/FASD in the neonatal period 270

Book reviews

Foetal Alcohol Spectrum Disorders: Parenting a child with an invisible disability
by Julia Brown and Dr Mary Mather 275
Reviewed by Rena Phillips

Assessing Disorganized Attachment Behaviour in Children
by David Shemmings and Yvonne Shemmings 277
Reviewed by Stuart Harragan

Promoting the Health of Children in Public Care
by Florence Merredew and Carolyn Sampeys 278
Reviewed by Jean Harris-Hendriks

Abstracts 280

Accessing the journal

Adoption & Fostering is co-published by Sage Publications and the CoramBAAF Adoption & Fostering Academy. This follows a transfer of services in August 2015 from the former charity that was BAAF (British Association for Adoption and Fostering) to the Coram group, resulting in the formation of the new entity, CoramBAAF.

Until further notice, individual and corporate members of CoramBAAF will gain access via the usual links in the Members' area of the former BAAF website: www.baaf.org.uk. Members will continue to enjoy online access to *Adoption & Fostering* articles back to 1977, as well as the additional benefit of free access to the *Journal of Social Work* back to 2001.

Glossary of terms

Adoption & Fostering
2015, Vol. 39(3) 195–196

DOI: 10.1177/0308575915599121
adoptionfostering.sagepub.com

Attention Deficit Hyperactivity Disorder (ADHD)
A group of behavioural symptoms that include inattentiveness, hyperactivity and impulsiveness. ADHD can occur in people of any intellectual ability, although it is more common in those with learning difficulties.

Agenesis of the corpus callosum (ACC)
Congenital birth defect characterised by complete or partial absence of the structure that connects the two hemispheres of the brain – the corpus callosum – which is the largest fibre tract in the central nervous system.

Canthus
Either corner of the eye where the upper and lower eyelids meet.

Epidermolysis bullosa
General term used to describe a group of rare inherited skin disorders that cause the skin to become very fragile.

Facial phenotype
Observable facial traits resulting from the interaction of a person's genetic make-up with environmental factors, e.g. prenatal exposure to alcohol.

Foetal Alcohol Syndrome (FAS)
A collection of conditions, each of which includes a spectrum of severity, characterised by damage to the central nervous system and/or growth problems arising from prenatal exposure to alcohol. FAS involves some specific elements, such as facial features, most apparent in younger children.

Foetal Alcohol Spectrum Disorders (FASD)
Umbrella term used to describe the range of effects that can occur in an individual whose mother drank alcohol during pregnancy. These effects may include physical, mental, behavioural and/or learning disabilities with possible life-long implications.

Foetal Hydantoin Syndrome
A disorder caused by exposure of a foetus to phenytoin, a drug commonly prescribed for epilepsy.

Foetal Valproate Syndrome
A rare congenital disorder caused by exposure of the foetus to valproic acid during the first three months of pregnancy. Valproic acid is an anticonvulsant drug used to control certain types of seizures in the treatment of epilepsy.

Hemiplegia
A life-long condition that causes weakness or complete paralysis of one side of the body and is caused by injury to parts of the brain that control movements of the limbs, trunk, face, etc. This can happen before, during or after birth. The condition can be congenital or acquired.

Maternal phenylketonuria
A mother with the rare genetic disease phenylketonuria (PKU) whose high blood levels of phenylalanine (phe) are dangerous to a developing foetus. High phe is a teratogen. It can damage a baby before birth.

Microcephaly
Rare neurological condition in which an infant's head is significantly smaller than those of other children of the same age and sex. Sometimes detected at birth, microcephaly usually results from the brain developing abnormally in the womb or not growing as it should after birth.

Myelination
Myelination is the process by which a fatty layer called myelin accumulates around nerve cells (neurons). Myelin particularly forms around the long shaft, or axon, of neurons. Myelination enables nerve cells to transmit information faster and allows for more complex brain processes, so the process is vitally important to the healthy functioning of the central nervous system.

Myotonia syndrome
A symptom of a small number of certain neuromuscular disorders characterised by delayed relaxation (prolonged contraction) of the skeletal muscles after voluntary contraction or electrical stimulation. It causes muscle stiffness that interferes with movement.

Neonatal Abstinence Syndrome (NAS)
A group of problems that occur in a newborn who was exposed to addictive opiate drugs in the mother's womb.

Palpebral fissure measurement
Measuring the distance from the endocanthion (the point at which the inner ends of the upper and lower eyelid meet) to the exocanthion (the outer corner of the eye fissure where the eyelids meet).

Philtrum
Area of the upper face between the nose and the lips.

adoption
&fostering

Editorial

The invisible disability

Mary Mather

Adoption & Fostering
2015, Vol. 39(3) 197–200

DOI: 10.1177/0308575915594983
adoptionfostering.sagepub.com
SAGE

The issue of excessive alcohol consumption in the UK has long been salient in debates about public health and social morals. Although concern was common before the Industrial Revolution, Hogarth's *Gin Lane* published in 1751 painted a graphic picture of the social disorder that followed the availability of cheap gin, and worries escalated with the expansion of cities after 1820. Temperance movements mushroomed around the 1860s, fuelled by the teachings of Evangelistic religion and social reformers like Joseph Rowntree. However, the difference between then and now is that the perceived harm was on family life – principally the neglect of children and domestic violence – and after 1914 the impact on industrial production during the two world wars. There was no notion of damage to the unborn child.

Over the last 40 years however, it has been conclusively established that exposure to alcohol before birth is the most important preventable cause of brain damage in children that could affect up to one in every 100 babies in England and Wales. This means that about 7000 affected infants are born every year, more than the combined total of children born with Down's syndrome, cerebral palsy, Sudden Infant Death Syndrome (SIDS), cystic fibrosis and spina bifida. The effects of exposure range from devastating physical and learning disabilities to subtle damage causing impulsive behaviour, violence and criminality. The situation is all the more tragic because the condition is 100% preventable, lifelong and untreatable. The cost to society, as well as to the individuals and their families, is staggering.

Why is it that despite all that is now known about alcohol, health and social care professionals are still not particularly well-informed in this area? In contrast to other developed countries, in England and Wales there is still widespread denial of the importance of the problem. In the USA, the Surgeon General first advised women not to drink in pregnancy as early as 1981. Current US guidance states that there is no known safe amount of alcohol to drink while pregnant, no safe time to drink and no safe kind of alcohol. Pregnant women in Canada, Denmark, France, Norway, Israel, Mexico, Australia, Ireland, New Zealand, Spain, the Netherlands and Scotland are now advised to abstain completely from alcohol. Why is there such reluctance to support this growing international consensus?

The UK has a relatively light touch system of regulation compared to many developed countries. Liberalising the licensing laws has led to intense competition among retailers, driving down supermarket prices and shifting consumption away from pubs into the home. Major sporting events are propped up by generous alcohol sponsorship and the link between alcohol and sport, both on and off the pitch, is well ingrained in the British psyche. The UK, with the exception of Scotland, is the only EU member apart from Malta to maintain a drink driving blood alcohol limit of 80mgs. The result is a regulatory system that totally fails to protect the vulnerable and children.

A recent search for the term 'fetal alcohol'[1] in an archive of worldwide medical publications produced more than 14,500 articles. Virtually none of them emanated from the UK and to highlight what is happening here has not been an easy task. This lack of research and definitive guidance in the UK has led to unconsidered and diverse opinions about alcohol, where every professional has a different view and pregnant women are left confused and uncertain.

There is no doubt that significant numbers of British women are drinking in pregnancy to a level that puts their babies at risk. A recent UK prospective study showed that the percentage of women drinking alcohol during pregnancy was 79%, 63% and 49%, for the first, second and third trimesters respectively (Nykjaer, 2014). Few of these women were considered to be problem drinkers. The same study showed that the pregnant woman most likely to drink was over 35, in a managerial or professional occupation and from a white ethnic background.

Even more concerning are the pregnant women whose children are removed because they are chronically dependent on alcohol and/or drugs. These children face the complexities of life in care with the added burden that their disabilities due to alcohol are largely unrecognised. The articles in this special edition make it clear that these children pose a huge challenge to our services. There is an urgent need to recognise prenatal alcohol exposure at an early stage and to develop pathways for diagnosis, assessment and support.

Early diagnosis is the key to the future successful management of the affected child. Diagnosis is not easy as most of the contributors to this journal describe. It depends not on a single test, but upon obtaining and assessing information in four areas. This is not simply a health-based task but one which must be shared between health and social care.

The first and most crucial element of the diagnosis is a history of exposure to alcohol before birth. For the looked after child, this information can be almost impossible to obtain because it is not routinely documented by children's services. Accurate information about maternal alcohol, unlike illegal drugs, is rarely documented in either the child's medical or social care records. Confidentiality prevents access to maternal records once the child has moved out of the birth family. Social care records are lost as workers come and go, cases are transferred between teams and adopted and fostered children leave the local area. As a result most looked after children with alcohol-induced brain damage will have the catastrophic learning and behaviour problems, but will never receive a formal diagnosis.

The second area needed for diagnosis is a history of poor growth before and after birth. This is also a difficult area to evaluate for the looked after child. Other factors in their lives, such as maternal cigarette smoking and drugs, poor antenatal care, neglect, poor nutrition and multiple placement moves, can cause faltering growth. In addition, early weights may have not been recorded or centile charts not filled in or the parent-held record lost. Only the most severely affected children, those with foetal alcohol syndrome (FAS), will have poor growth. A significant number of affected children, those with a foetal alcohol spectrum disorder (FASD), will have normal growth parameters.

The third area, the characteristic facial features, are often incorrectly relied on to make a diagnosis in the absence of other information. But these features – a short palpebral fissure (small eyes), flat or smooth philtrum and a thin upper lip – are caused by exposure to alcohol while the face is forming in the first six weeks of pregnancy. If the mother does not drink alcohol in this period, the face will be normal and once it is formed the child's features will not change.

The vast majority (over 85%) of children damaged from prenatal alcohol exposure have no physical birth defects. They have normal faces and normal growth but will exhibit the devastating cognitive and behavioural difficulties caused by alcohol exposure in the last three months of pregnancy. This is usually the main reason for referring the child for diagnosis. Such children exhibit numerous signs and symptoms: hyperactivity, impulsiveness, short memory spans, difficulty concentrating, poor planning and organisational skills, poor judgement and failure to consider the consequences of their actions, motor problems, speech and language difficulties, perceptual disorders, and specific learning disabilities. This is because they have generalised organic brain damage caused by alcohol exposure that affects the executive functioning of the pre-frontal cortex, as described by Bill Phillips in this journal. These difficulties can be as severe in the child without facial features as in one with a diagnostic face. They may not be evident until early school age when the prenatal alcohol exposure is forgotten or considered irrelevant.

Affected children are usually given multiple inaccurate diagnoses. Many are identified as having ADHD, atypical autism, an attachment disorder or a conduct disorder. As Brian Roberts illustrates here, all have trouble coping in school. The children are often taken from professional to professional, accumulating diagnoses as they grow older. Families and social workers are often on a 'diagnostic merry-go-round' in the vain hope that a new prognosis will explain the child's difficulties and provide a 'cure' for their problems. Placements with adoptive and foster families can break down because of the challenges they present. Julia Brown's article describes the challenges of caring for the affected child, the incorrect advice given to parents and carers and the absence of effective services.

There are undoubtedly large numbers of unrecognised and affected children in the care system. Geraldine Gregory's local audit found that 34% of children referred to her for looked after children health assessments and 75% of children referred for adoption medicals had a history of prenatal alcohol exposure. Diagnostic services are patchy across the country and a postcode lottery operates. Few places have the gold standard multidisciplinary assessment team which is routine in the USA and Canada. Raja Mukherjee and colleagues look at professional knowledge and attitudes in this country and the stigma that can still be associated with diagnosis while Maggie Watts describes work being carried out in Scotland in terms of diagnosis and professional training.

Attachment theory has dominated child care practice in the UK and the concept of behaviour due to organic untreatable brain damage is new to most health and social care professionals. The UK is the binge drinking capital of Europe and 50% of pregnancies are unplanned; every day that alcohol is ignored or downplayed, more damaged babies are being born. There is an urgent need for action and research.

More data are needed about the prevalence of FASD both in the general population and among those 'looked after'. Clear national guidelines about totally avoiding alcohol during pregnancy are essential. There needs to be mandatory labelling on all alcoholic products highlighting the risks of drinking while pregnant. The recording of accurate information about maternal lifestyles in pregnancy must become routine social work practice. Protocols need to be established which ensure that the information is then transferred to the child's record. Adopters must be given clear facts about maternal lifestyles in pregnancy that could have implications for their child's future. Many more diagnostic clinics are needed with doctors with the expertise to run them. Training for midwives, social workers, doctors, foster carers and others in preventing and managing FASD is essential. Respite care needs to be made available for children who look normal and who have no obvious disability.

In terms of influencing drinking cultures in the UK, public health professionals face huge obstacles. They have to attack two deeply entrenched cultural attitudes. One is that large sections of British society believe that the only way of having a good time is to get completely intoxicated. Too many individuals believe that definition of a 'great night out' is the one 'no one can remember' the next day. The second is that throughout history, from Shakespeare, to music hall, to reality TV, drunkenness is seen as funny in a way that drug use or smoking is not. There is also a need to differentiate between types of drinking behaviour. Strategies to reduce the impact of social disorder at weekends are unlikely to be effective for the individual who drinks alone at home every night. There are no simple approaches to the problem. Restricting the supply and availability of alcohol combined with an increase in the price has been shown to reduce the harm inflicted on society, but these draconian measures are unlikely to be acceptable to the public or to politicians and would be strenuously fought by the global, very powerful alcohol conglomerates.

FASD is a lifelong disability but it is not life shortening. If every pregnant woman stopped drinking today there would be no new cases, but society would still have to provide 80 years of care for a group of highly damaged individuals who were born with an invisible disability over which they had no control.

Note

1. The spelling of foetus/foetal varies across the world. While this version is more usual in the UK and will be used in this journal, it is advisable to use the more common spellings of fetus/fetal when searching for resources on the internet.

Reference

Nykjaer C, Alwan NA, Greenwood DC, Simpson NA, Hay AW, White KL and Cade JE (2014) Maternal alcohol intake prior to and during pregnancy and risk of adverse birth outcomes: evidence from a British cohort. *Journal of Epidemiology & Community Health* 68: 542–549.

Dr Mary Mather is a retired Community Paediatric Consultant with a special interest in FASD. She is a Trustee of the FASD Trust and co-author of *Foetal Alcohol Spectrum Disorders: Parenting a child with an invisible disability* (FASD Trust, 2014).

Article

Prenatal exposure to alcohol causes enduring brain damage

Adoption & Fostering
2015, Vol. 39(3) 201–211

DOI: 10.1177/0308575915597875
adoptionfostering.sagepub.com

WA Phillips
University of Stirling, Scotland, UK

Abstract

This article summarises recent discoveries showing how prenatal exposure to alcohol affects the structure and function of the brain and of the individual neurons from which it is built. It explains why this weakens the ability to select activities that are appropriate in the context of current circumstances. It also explains why this reduces the ability to suppress habitual, automatic or impulsive responses when they are inappropriate. These effects of alcohol on the brain lead to enduring impairments in cognition, planning and self-control that become more obvious at later stages of child development. The complexities of these processes and the limitations of current knowledge are acknowledged. The article concludes that many of the enduring cognitive, emotional and social impairments associated with prenatal exposure to alcohol are the expected consequences of the effects that such exposure is known to have on the developing brain.

Keywords

FASD, alcohol-related neurodevelopmental defects, prenatal alcohol, executive function disability, brain development, cortical neurons

Introduction

This article provides an introduction to recent research on the neurobiological bases of the enduring effects on brain function of prenatal exposure to alcohol. Given the host of other risk factors and adverse conditions likely to affect adopted and fostered children, why should this journal devote a whole issue to foetal alcohol spectrum disorders (FASD)? Dr Mary Mather offers some answers to this question in her editorial. In addition, those most relevant to this opening contribution can be listed as follows:

1. Exposure to alcohol is one of the most common risk factors to which adopted and fostered children are subjected.

Corresponding author:
Bill Phillips, Division of Psychology, School of Natural Sciences, University of Stirling, FK9 4LA, Scotland, UK.
Email: wap1@stir.ac.uk

2. It is, in principle, entirely preventable by not drinking during pregnancy and this opportunity to prevent it will be more widely taken if the effects of prenatal alcohol exposure are more widely known.
3. Diagnosis is difficult and in many cases there are no obvious problems until later in development. This delay makes it hard to distinguish the effects of FASD from neglectful parenting or a host of other risk factors, thus producing unjustified feelings of guilt or inadequacy in adoptive or foster parents. If they were informed of the cognitive impairments associated with FASD, they would be in a far better position to assess and adjust their parenting accordingly.
4. As Mather notes, the UK lags behind other developed countries in research on FASD and there is reluctance in the UK to accept the growing international consensus on its importance.
5. The consequences of FASD for cognitive development are complex and highly variable across individuals and the evidence from cognitive neuroscience makes it clear why this is so.

To unravel these complexities it is necessary to build on a firm empirical base, such as that provided by the research outlined below. This research cannot be restricted to studies of humans because pregnant women cannot be randomly divided into two groups, one being made to drink alcohol during and only during pregnancy and the other being prevented from doing so at any time. However, such rigorously controlled studies have been performed on non-human animals, leading to the finding that prenatal exposure to alcohol impairs neuronal structures and processes that are common to humans and other mammals. Furthermore, much of the damage occurs before many of the cognitive capabilities that are distinctively human have developed. Evidence for commonalities between the effects of alcohol on prenatal brain development in humans and in other animals is further provided by in-depth comparisons of its consequences for cognition and behaviour in both. Much remains to be discovered by making such comparisons, but the research highlighted here already shows that there are several similarities between the effects on cognition and behaviour in humans and in other animals. None of this implies that there are no relevant differences between the two groups. For example, there may well be management strategies for coping with the consequences of FASD that are only available via the use of language, so such strategies are necessarily limited to humans. Nevertheless, the impairments to be managed have occurred so early in the course of brain development, and they affect physiological processes that are so fundamental and which have been conserved throughout so much of evolutionary history, that it is highly unlikely that humans have immunity to them. Rigorously controlled studies of non-human animals therefore make a major contribution to this area of study.

Every human brain is an extraordinary creation in which endless variations are played on fundamental themes of life and mind. It is a perpetual construction site, ever changing from the first embryonic stages at which it begins to form until a few moments before death. Each is built from a large repertoire of neuronal components that are grown on site in a fluctuating biochemical and physiological climate, and the ongoing construction is flexibly adapted to unforeseeable circumstances as they occur. Human brains are built from more than 80 billion neurons, connected by more than 176,000 kilometres of myelinated axonal cables, via about 100 trillion adaptable connections called synapses. Minds are of course much more than a pile of neurons, just as a house is much more than a pile of bricks, but minds badly built and from deficient components are greatly disadvantaged, as are houses that are badly designed and constructed from deficient materials. Furthermore, although it has general long-term goals and guidelines for approaching them, brain construction occurs without anything analogous to an architect's drawing of the intended house, because there is no such thing as an 'intended' human brain. In addition to all of this, feedback on progress towards the long-term goals is ambiguous, partial and not wholly reliable. The feats performed by nature in creating such things as human brains are therefore truly awesome. Among the most impressive are the abilities by which we flexibly regulate the formation of our percepts, thoughts, emotions and actions so that they are well adapted to both current circumstances and long-term goals. These feats include the ability to attend purposefully to selected things while suppressing reactions to irrelevant distractions and controlling inappropriate impulses. At its best, this produces wise decisions that take lots of relevant information into account, including large amounts of personal, inter-personal and social information.

Abilities that help us do these things are built into the brain at both the level of specialised brain regions, such as that of the prefrontal cortex (PFC), and at the level of individual neurons, such as that of pyramidal neurons in the cortex. These neurons are called pyramidal because their cell bodies have approximately the shape of a pyramid, although the neuron as a whole is much more like that of a tall tree in which the trunk is called the apical dendrite and the roots the basal dendrites. Dendrites are the branch- and root-shaped parts of a neuron via which it receives signals from other neurons. Each neuron sends signals to thousands of others via a thin cable called the axon that emerges directly from their cell body. Pyramidal neurons are excitatory and constitute the workhorses of the cortex. They make up about 80% of all cortical neurons. The remaining neurons are mostly inhibitory, and both they and the pyramidal cells are affected by prenatal exposure to alcohol (Granato, 2006; Gruerri, Basinet and Riley, 2009).[1]

Given the huge difficulties faced by brain development and by its continuing adaptation throughout life, it should be no surprise that the processes by which this is achieved can go awry in so many different ways. I assume that few birth mothers would knowingly make those difficulties even greater. Therefore one aim of this article is to review the evidence showing that early exposure to alcohol does just that: it makes a near-impossible feat even harder. In addition to encouraging abstinence during pregnancy, an understanding of the enduring effects of prenatal exposure to alcohol on the brain may help guide the design of therapies and management strategies. It should also increase compassion for affected people and their carers, who have to grapple with those effects on a daily basis.

The terminology in current use to refer to brain damage due to prenatal exposure to alcohol is varied. FASD is one of the more commonly used terms, but can be misleading for at least three reasons. First, it is derived from the earlier term foetal alcohol syndrome (FAS). Facial deformations are the most obvious distinguishing characteristic of FAS, but they only occur when there have been unusually high levels of exposure during the first prenatal trimester, i.e. the first three months of gestation, which is when the face is being formed. The brain continues to develop throughout gestation and its growth can be harmed by levels of exposure below that required to produce facial deformations. It is therefore common for brain development to be affected by exposure to alcohol in the absence of any obvious effects on facial appearance. Second, classifying a disorder as FASD implies that there is a single dimension or spectrum of severity on which any particular individual can be placed. This is simply a convenient myth. The effects of exposure to alcohol during development vary from individual to individual in so many ways that they cannot be adequately characterised by any single measure of severity. Third, the notion of a single measure of severity suggests that there might be a safe level of exposure below which there is no harm. I know of no psychological or neurobiological evidence for the idea of a threshold below which there is no harm and above which there is a great deal. Alcohol-related neurodevelopmental defects (ARND) is a less used but more accurate description, hence the use of FASD/ARND as the umbrella term to refer to the broad class of effects with which this article is concerned.

People affected by FASD/ARND and their carers often report that being given the diagnosis changed the course of their lives for the better. This is because it helps them to understand the nature and cause of some of their disabilities and thus how to better deal with them. It is important to realise, however, that these disabilities vary widely from one person to the next, so that when such a diagnosis is given what is then needed is an insightful and individual understanding of its implications for that particular person.

The annual burden imposed by FASD/ARND on the healthcare budget of Canada, where the condition is well recognised and understood, has been estimated to be above $5 billion. Though it is not a major focus of research in the UK, a search for 'fetal alcohol' in *PubMed*, an archive of worldwide medical publications, recently retrieved more than 14,500 articles (Granato and De Giorgio, 2015). Even if my research were focused specifically on FASD/ARND, which it is not, it would be impossible for me to review more than a small fraction of so many publications. Instead, the central aim of this article is simply to show why that research strongly suggests that prenatal exposure to alcohol causes enduring brain damage. Although the term 'alcohol' is used throughout, it refers specifically to ethanol in the case of the rigorously controlled animal studies.

Evidence that symptoms of FASD/ARND are due to prenatal exposure to alcohol

As expected given its complexity, many things influence brain development, so how do we know that it is the alcohol that causes some of the cognitive, emotional and social difficulties associated with FASD/ARND and not other disadvantages? Many affected children are born into an environment of malnutrition and drug abuse, together with poor socio-economic lifestyles and neglectful parenting. It could be argued that these other factors are the cause of all or most of the symptoms of FASD/ARND. However, rigorous scientific studies have now dealt with the issue convincingly. As in the analogous case of smoking and lung cancer, epidemiological and other data provide strong circumstantial evidence against this argument. There is still room for doubt, but as with smoking and lung cancer, such uncertainties can be removed by experimental studies using non-human animals in which the relevant neuronal anatomy and physiology are sufficiently close to those of humans. Such studies now clearly show that exposure to alcohol in the early stages of brain development brings about enduring brain damage, and they have begun to outline the dosage and timing factors of alcohol use during pregnancy that contribute to variations in the brain damage and behavioural impairments caused (Guerri, et al., 2009). Species that have been used to study the effects of prenatal exposure to alcohol include non-human primates, but most of these studies have used rodents (Cudd, 2005). Rodents' brains, though smaller, are composed of neurons that are nearly indistinguishable from those of humans, so it is most likely that the effects observed in these animals apply to humans too. Those studies show that the effects caused can vary greatly from case to case, depending on many aspects of the individual and the exposure, such as the levels of alcohol reaching the foetal brain, the duration and pattern of exposure, and its timing relative to the stage of brain development. These factors all greatly influence the type and the extent of damage (Guerri, et al., 2009). One simple common finding is that the extent of the harm caused increases with the amount of alcohol to which the developing brain is exposed. In addition, the ability of the mother's and foetus's physiology to metabolise alcohol influences the risk of alcohol-induced defects. The specific brain structures affected and the magnitude of the damage are strongly influenced by the developmental timing of exposure. The facial feature deformities that are associated with FAS arise only when high blood-alcohol levels occur during early embryonic stages, such as the first trimester in humans but also applicable to mice and macaque monkeys (Guerri, Bazinet and Riley, 2009).

Exposure to alcohol affects brain development throughout all prenatal stages, but it influences different aspects of that development at different points. The damage caused by prenatal exposure to alcohol is therefore in some ways analogous to that resulting from a car crash in that there are endless variations on the exact type of damage, with no predictable pattern common to all. There is no evidence for a threshold in the amount of exposure to alcohol below which there is no damage. On the contrary, there is evidence that even 'moderate' amounts of exposure to alcohol can be harmful (e.g. Abate, et al., 2008; Valenzuela, et al., 2012). One way in which even low amounts of alcohol during the late stages of pregnancy can affect adult behaviour is by increasing the chances that that person will seek alcohol when an adult (Abate, et al., 2008; Spear and Molina, 2005). This is because preference for an environment containing alcohol can be passed on to the unborn foetus by low to moderate amounts of prenatal alcohol exposure. Thus, though there are well-established genetic variations in susceptibility to alcohol, this particular form of increased risk is due to the mother's drinking during pregnancy, not to her genes.

Cognitive, emotional and social consequences of FASD/ARND

The various cognitive, behavioural, emotional and social consequences of FASD/ARND are all too clear to those who live with them. The most salient difficulties involve impairments such as attentional disorders similar to attention deficit hyperactivity disorder (ADHD), impaired learning and memory, and a reduced ability to suppress inappropriate impulsive reactions. Some of the most pervasive impairments involve executive function, emotional control and self-regulation, which seem to be intractable features that persist throughout life (Soh, et al., 2015). Mathematical abilities and fine motor co-ordination are also frequently impaired. Given such an extensive list of impairments it is clear that the effects of alcohol on brain development are widely spread throughout the brain.

As the most rigorous scientific studies of the effects of prenatal alcohol on cognition and behaviour are carried out on animals, it is necessary to show that valid comparisons can be made between the behavioural consequences in animals and the symptoms of FASD/ARND in humans. Ways in which this has been done are reviewed in depth by Patten, Fontaine and Christie (2014). They show that impairments of executive function, one of the hallmarks of higher cognitive deficits in FASD/ARND, also occur in experimental animals exposed to alcohol under rigorously controlled experimental conditions. Executive functioning has been broadly defined as the ability to regulate attention and to use appropriate problem-solving abilities. More specifically, it includes such things as the ability to ignore distractions, the ability to suppress automatic but inappropriate reactions, working memory abilities and the capacity to flexibly switch cognitive strategies in response to current goals and conditions. These functions are in part dependent on frontal lobe structures such as the prefrontal cortex. In humans, they can be rigorously measured through standardised tests, such as the Stroop task in which the automatic tendency to read a word such as 'yellow' must be suppressed in favour of naming the colour of the ink in which it is printed. All such tests of executive function show it to be impaired in FASD/ARND. Other fundamental capabilities that are known to be impaired, such as fine motor skills, the control of attention, learning and memory and social skills, have also been shown to be impaired in animals that were exposed to alcohol during the early stages of brain development (Chokroborty-Hoque, Alberry and Singh, 2014; Patten, Fontaine and Christie, 2014). It is therefore highly likely that the effects of prenatal alcohol on the behaviour of animals in these experiments are relevant to the effects of FASD/ARND on cognition and behaviour as seen in humans.

Effects of prenatal alcohol on regional brain structure and function

Brain imaging, neurobiological and psychological studies have all been used to identify the specific brain regions affected by FASD/ARND. Neuro-imaging studies in humans have demonstrated reductions in the size of the brain as a whole, and particularly of specific regions of the cerebral cortex such as the prefrontal cortex and regions of the parietal lobe (which are central to executive function and attention), the amygdala (which is central to anxiety and other emotions) and the cerebellum (which plays important roles in cognition and in co-ordinating actions such as those involved in fine motor control) (Guerri, et al., 2009; Riley and McGee, 2005; Soh, et al., 2015). These studies show that it is not only the gross anatomical size of these brain regions that is impaired; they also reveal that their activities as measured by functional neuro-imaging are affected, sometimes being less than that in control groups and sometimes more. Cases where activity of prefrontal regions is greater than normal suggest that people with FASD/ARND often have to work harder to achieve what others can do with much less effort. They have to work harder because they have to take much of the current contextual information into account by conscious voluntary effort. For people unaffected by FASD/ARND, much more of this information is absorbed automatically, thus requiring less voluntary effort.

Overall, it is clear that although regions concerned with higher mental functions are particularly vulnerable, the damage caused by prenatal alcohol is widespread throughout the brain and is not restricted to just a few regions. This is to be expected given that some of the damaging effects occur before the various brain regions are well differentiated. The following section therefore reviews the evidence showing that it is not only the overall architecture of the brain that is affected but also the structure and function of the very components from which it is built, i.e. the individual brain cells.

Effects of prenatal alcohol on the glial cells and pyramidal neurons of the cerebral cortex

Recent studies have clearly implicated glial cells in FASD/ARND as well as in some other neurodevelopmental disorders including Down's syndrome, Fragile X syndrome and Autism Spectrum Disorders (Guerri, Basinet and Riley, 2009; Guizzetti, et al., 2014). Glial cells guide neuronal growth and are found throughout the whole cortex. Abnormalities of these cells therefore have wide-ranging effects. Although they are not central to moment-by-moment processing of information in the brain, glial cells play a central role in guiding the development, survival and function of pyramidal neurons during the early stages of brain development and beyond. Alterations in glial cell function thus have major consequences for adult brain architecture, connectivity and function. The changes in brain structure and function that are characteristic of FASD/ARND include a greatly reduced number of pyramidal cells in the cerebral cortex and malformation of the corpus callosum, which is the thick band of axonal cables that connects the left and right cortical hemispheres. These are expected consequences of the glial cell malfunctions known to be caused by exposure to alcohol (Guerri, Pascual and Renau-Piqueras, 2001; Guerri, et al., 2009; Guizzetti, et al., 2014).

In both humans and other animals the cerebral cortex is one of the brain regions most affected by FASD, and when exposed to alcohol during prenatal development cortical neurons are subject to an increased rate of pruning or cell death (Guerri, Basinet and Riley, 2009). Furthermore, the surviving neurons have enduring impairments (e.g. Granato, et al., 2003; Miller, et al., 1990). Recent work now clearly shows that exposure to alcohol during the early stages of brain development leads to enduring impairment of the structure and function of the pyramidal neurons of which the cortex is mostly composed (Granato, et al., 2012). This work is important because it helps to explain the particular pattern of cognitive, emotional and social impairments seen in FASD/ARND. It shows that the neuronal mechanisms particularly impaired by early exposure to alcohol include those concerned with regulating neuronal activity so that it is well adapted to the particular needs of the moment. These mechanisms involve synaptic connections that are made on specific parts of pyramidal neurons, i.e. on their apical dendrites. It is those connections in particular that were found to be much reduced in rats exposed to alcohol at a developmental stage equivalent to the third trimester in humans (De Giorgio and Granato, 2015). Those connections play a central role in regulating neuronal activity because they amplify local neuron activities that are relevant in the context of current activity elsewhere in the brain. Inappropriate activities can be suppressed by inhibiting this amplification. Such neuronal mechanisms have been known to cellular neurophysiologists for several years (e.g. Larkum, Zhu and Sakmann, 1999), but their crucial role in the cognitive functions that are impaired by exposure to alcohol during early development are only now becoming clear (Larkum, 2013; Phillips, Clark and Silverstein, 2015). Further understanding of these mechanisms, their role in mental life and their impairments in FASD/ARND may therefore make it possible to design coping and therapeutic strategies that are more effective than those currently available.

Therapeutic strategies in relation to the underlying neuronal bases of FASD/ARND

Since FASD/ARND was first identified there have been several attempts to identify effective interventions that reduce its adverse consequences. These efforts are encouraged by findings showing that affected adults have fewer secondary disabilities if they are diagnosed, and presumably more appropriately treated, early in life (Streissguth, et al., 2004). Although most strategies for managing or ameliorating the consequences of FASD/ARND have not been clearly related to its underlying neuronal bases, a few have been. Wells and colleagues (2012) evaluated the effectiveness of 'neurocognitive habilitation', a group therapy intervention adapted for use by foster and adoptive caregivers and their children who were prenatally exposed to alcohol. The therapeutic intervention used combined techniques and interventions developed to treat cases of traumatic brain injury with components of the Alert programme (Williams and Shellenberger, 1996). This programme helps children improve self-regulatory skills by teaching them how to identify their arousal level and how to alter it on the basis of current situational demands. In particular, the intervention sought to teach the children how to identify internal indicators of dysregulation and how to use strategies to improve their self-regulation and emotional control within the context of complex group settings, such as those they have to deal with at home and at school. Wells and colleagues' (2012) findings provided evidence of the effectiveness of the intervention in improving executive functioning and emotional problem-solving in children with FASD/ARND. Soh and colleagues (2015) have now combined the use of this therapy with brain scans done both before and after the intervention. They also found evidence of the same kind of behavioural improvements as did Wells, et al. (2012), but, in addition, they discovered that the brain regions most enhanced by the treatment were those prefrontal and other cortical regions that support functions such as response inhibition and emotional control, which the intervention sought to improve.

There is also evidence that although there are as yet no therapies that fully overcome the impairments associated with FASD/ARND, they can be ameliorated by an enriched environment involving rich physical, cognitive and social experiences (Kodituwakku, 2010; Peadon, et al., 2009). Animal experiments have recently shown that being raised in an enriched environment can ameliorate some of the deficits produced in mice by early exposure to alcohol. Compared to small non-enriched cages and a basic food supply, enriched cages are larger, with toys of various shapes, sizes and textures, tunnels, nesting material, heavy bedding and access to running wheels and ladders. Being raised in such an enriched environment reduced anxiety and produced long-lasting improvements in learning and memory in mice exposed to alcohol as well as in those that were not (Chokroborty-Hoque, Alberry and Singh, 2014). Social enrichment, i.e. housing ethanol-exposed rats with non-exposed control rats, has been shown to partially reverse some of the adverse effects of early exposure to alcohol in adult rats (Middleton, Varlinskaya and Mooney, 2012). The adverse effects of alcohol and the beneficial effects of social enrichment in those experiments were assessed by behavioural measures such as social investigation (sniffing the other rat's body), contact behaviour (grooming, crawling over or under the novel rat), play fighting (following, chasing, nape attacks, pinning), and social motivation (a ratio of social preference vs. avoidance of the other rat). The most significant finding was that prenatal ethanol exposure impaired social motivation performance in both male and female rats, and that this impairment was reversed by social enrichment.

Conclusions

It is clear that in our society, exposure to alcohol is one of the major risk factors faced by the human brain during prenatal development. The brain damage caused can have consequences that endure well into adult life. The repercussions for cognition, emotion and social behaviour are clear to all of those who live with them. This damage affects brain function on both large and small scales. On the large scale of brain size and organisation it results in smaller brains with those regions that are concerned with the overall organisation and regulation of neuronal activity and behaviour, such as the prefrontal cortex, being particularly vulnerable. However, the effects of prenatal alcohol are not only limited to these large-scale effects. It is not just the structure of the brain as a whole that is affected; there is also an impact on the structure and function of the neurons from which the neocortex is built, i.e. pyramidal cells and inhibitory interneurons. The various symptoms of FASD/ARND are as expected given the nature of those effects on both the large and the small scales. This leaves little room for doubt concerning the causal role of prenatal exposure to alcohol in producing cognitive impairments in adults. Although there is evidence that these effects can be managed and ameliorated by appropriate strategies, they make life much more difficult for those concerned. By increasing the overall amount of such exposure, the drinking 'culture' of societies such as the UK bears a heavy burden of responsibility. In the long term this burden may be lightened by cultural changes that reduce the amount of prenatal exposure to alcohol, e.g. by informing people of the facts and by putting prominent warnings on alcoholic products. In the meantime, society needs to provide support, therapy and understanding for those exceptional people who bear the burden most directly, i.e. affected individuals and those who care for them.

Acknowledgements

First, I must thank my wife Rena for educating me on the concrete daily realities faced by families who have to deal with the consequences of prenatal exposure to alcohol. I must also thank her for suggesting that I write this article and for making many useful suggestions as to how the presentation could be improved. Thanks are also due to Alberto Granato, a leading international authority on experimental studies of FASD, who, over the course of two days of intensive discussion, greatly strengthened the scientific case presented here. I am also grateful to two anonymous reviewers whose comments were used to improve the article.

Note

1. For a short and simple introduction to the effects of psychoactive drugs, including alcohol, on the brain see Phillips (2004). For a review focused specifically on the effects of prenatal alcohol see Plant (2004). Both of these reviews are included in the BAAF anthology *Children Exposed to Parental Substance Misuse: Implications for family placement* (Phillips, 2004). Many of the scientific studies of prenatal alcohol reviewed below were performed after they were written. For an in-depth practical guide to parenting children with FASD see Brown and Mather (2014) reviewed in this journal.

References

Abate P, Pueta M, Spear NE and Molina JC (2008) Fetal learning about ethanol and later ethanol responsiveness: evidence against 'safe' amounts of prenatal exposure. *Experimental Biology and Medicine* 233(2): 139–154.

Brown J and Mather M (2014) *Foetal Alcohol Spectrum Disorders: Parenting a child with an invisible disability*. Oxford: FASD Trust.

Chokroborty-Hoque A, Alberry B and Singh SM (2014) Exploring the complexity of intellectual disability in fetal alcohol spectrum disorders. *Frontiers in Pediatrics* 2: 90.

Cudd TA (2005) Animal model systems for the study of alcohol teratology. *Experimental Biology and Medicine* 230(6): 389–393.

De Giorgio A and Granato A (2015) Reduced density of dendritic spines in pyramidal neurons of rats exposed to alcohol during early postnatal life. *International Journal of Developmental Neuroscience* 41: 74–79.

Granato A (2006) Altered organization of cortical interneurons in rats exposed to ethanol during neonatal life. *Brain Research* 1069(1): 23–30.

Granato A, Di Rocco F, Zumbo A, Toesca A and Giannetti S (2003) Organization of cortico-cortical associative projections in rats exposed to ethanol during early postnatal life. *Brain Research Bulletin* 60(4): 339–344.

Granato A, Palmer LM, De Giorgio A, Tavian D and Larkum ME (2012) Early exposure to alcohol leads to permanent impairment of dendritic excitability in neocortical pyramidal neurons. *The Journal of Neuroscience* 32(4): 1377–1382.

Guerri C, Bazinet A and Riley EP (2009) Foetal alcohol spectrum disorders and alterations in brain and behaviour. *Alcohol and Alcoholism* 44(2): 108–114.

Guerri C, Pascual M and Renau-Piqueras J (2001) Glia and fetal alcohol syndrome. *Neurotoxicology* 22(5): 593–599.

Guizzetti M, Zhang X, Goeke C and Gavin DP (2014) Glia and neurodevelopment: focus on fetal alcohol spectrum disorders. *Frontiers in Pediatrics* 2: 123.

Kodituwakku PW (2010) A neurodevelopmental framework for the development of interventions for children with fetal alcohol spectrum disorders. *Alcohol* 44(7–8): 717–28.

Larkum M (2013) A cellular mechanism for cortical associations: an organizing principle for the cerebral cortex. *Trends Neurosci* 36(3): 141–151.

Larkum ME, Zhu JJ and Sakmann B (1999) A new cellular mechanism for coupling inputs arriving at different cortical layers. *Nature* 398: 338–341.

Middleton FA, Varlinskaya EI and Mooney SM (2012) Molecular substrates of social avoidance seen following prenatal ethanol exposure and its reversal by social enrichment. *Developmental Neuroscience* 34(2–3): 115–128.

Miller MW, Chiaia NL and Rhoades RW (1990) Intracellular recording and injection study of corticospinal neurons in the rat somatosensory cortex: effect of prenatal exposure to ethanol. *Journal of Comparative Neurology* 297(1): 91–105.

Patten AR, Fontaine CJ and Christie BR (2014) A comparison of the different animal models of fetal alcohol spectrum disorders and their use in studying complex behaviors. *Frontiers in Pediatrics* 2: 93.

Peadon E, Rhys-Jones B, Bower C and Elliott EJ (2009) Systematic review of interventions for children with fetal alcohol spectrum disorders. *BMC Pediatrics* 9: 35.

Phillips R (ed.) (2004) *Children Exposed to Parental Substance Misuse: Implications for family placement*. London: BAAF.

Phillips WA (2004) A brief introduction to the effects of psychoactive drugs. In: Phillips R (ed.) *Children Exposed to Parental Substance Misuse: Implications for family placement*. London: BAAF, pp. 30–40.

Phillips WA, Clark A and Silverstein SM (2015) On the functions, mechanisms, and malfunctions of intracortical contextual modulation. *Neuroscience and Biobehavioral Reviews* 52(1): 1–20.

Plant M (2004) Parental alcohol misuse: implications for child placement. In: Phillips R (ed.) *Children Exposed to Parental Substance Misuse: Implications for family placement*. London: BAAF, pp. 73–85.

Riley EP and McGee CL (2005) Fetal alcohol spectrum disorders: an overview with emphasis on changes in brain and behavior. *Experimental Biology and Medicine (Maywood)* 230(6): 357–365.

Soh DW, Skocic J, Nash K, Stevens S, Turner GR and Rovet J (2015) Self-regulation therapy increases frontal gray matter in children with fetal alcohol spectrum disorder: evaluation by voxel-based morphometry. *Frontiers in Human Neuroscience* 9: 108.

Spear NE and Molina JC (2005) Fetal or infantile exposure to ethanol promotes ethanol ingestion in adolescence and adulthood: a theoretical review. *Alcohol Clinical and Experimental Research* 29(6): 909–929.

Streissguth AP, Bookstein FL, Barr HM, Sampson PD, O'Malley K and Young JK (2004) Risk factors for adverse life outcomes in fetal alcohol syndrome and fetal alcohol effects. *Journal of Developmental and Behavioral Pediatrics* 25(4): 228–238.

Valenzuela CF, Morton RA, Diaz MR and Topper L (2012) Does moderate drinking harm the fetal brain? Insights from animal models. *Trends in Neurosciences* 35(5): 284–292.

Wells AM, Chasnoff IJ, Schmidt CA, Telford E and Schwartz LD (2012) Neurocognitive habilitation therapy for children with fetal alcohol spectrum disorders: an adaptation of the Alert Program. *American Journal of Occupational Therapy* 66: 24–34.

Williams MS and Shellenberger S (1996) *'How does your engine run?' A leader's guide to the Alert Program for self-regulation*. Albuquerque, NM: Therapy Works.

Bill Phillips is an Emeritus Professor, cognitive psychologist and theoretical neuroscientist in the Division of Psychology, School of Natural Sciences, University of Stirling, Scotland, UK.

Article

Knowledge and opinions of professional groups concerning FASD in the UK

Adoption & Fostering
2015, Vol. 39(3) 212–224

DOI: 10.1177/0308575915598931
adoptionfostering.sagepub.com

Raja Mukherjee
Specialist FASD Behavioural Clinic, UK

Elizabeth Wray
Specialist FASD Behavioural Clinic, UK

Leopold Curfs
Maastricht University Medical Center, Netherlands

Sheila Hollins
St George's University of London, UK

Abstract

While information from other countries suggests varying degrees of knowledge about foetal alcohol spectrum disorders (FASD), understanding of the condition among UK health professionals is unclear. This mixed methodology study aims to ascertain the UK picture. It comprised a standardised FASD questionnaire completed by 505 professionals and focus groups using semi-structured interviews. Among those professionals who attended focus groups, five broad themes were identified: lack of knowledge: need for consistent guidance; stigma: need for early intervention; and need for support services. The study highlights a need for training and improved recognition by professionals. Reluctance to diagnose could be due to associated stigma and therefore not merely reflect lack of knowledge. As an avoidable disorder the importance of prevention, as well as early identification of FASD to avert secondary disabilities such as mental health issues, highlights the need for specialist diagnostic and support services.

Keywords

FAS, FASD, knowledge, professionals, UK

Corresponding author:
Raja Mukherjee, FASD Specialist Behaviour Clinic, Bracketts Resource Centre, 116–118 Station Road East, Oxted RH8 0QA, UK.
Email: raja.mukherjee@sabp.nhs.uk

Introduction

FASD represents a group of disorders caused by prenatal alcohol exposure to a developing foetus (BMA Board of Science, 2007). The management of the condition can be separated into two broad areas: prevention and management (Mukherjee, Hollins and Turk, 2006). This requires health professionals to recognise both the risk in pregnant women and the presentation of the condition in children. When FASD is not recognised, the rates of secondary disability such as mental health problems have been shown to be high (Gray and Mukherjee, 2007). A wide range of health professionals are involved in FASD, from doctors and health visitors who give advice, to social workers working regularly with birth mothers and their children where FASD may be an outcome (Mukherjee, Hollins and Turk, 2006). The day-to-day prevention of such disorders falls primarily to obstetricians, midwives and family physicians, whereas the recognition of those affected is mainly the remit of paediatricians, psychiatrists, social workers, family physicians and health visitors. These are all supported by public health (Gray and Mukherjee, 2007; Mukherjee, Hollins and Turk, 2006).

Methods of inferring levels of knowledge among UK professionals, for example by rates of FASD diagnosis, have been found to underestimate expected prevalence (Morleo, et al., 2011) when compared with the findings of international studies (May, et al., 2009; Petkovic and Barisic, 2010). Thus the accuracy and extent of professional knowledge in the UK remains unclear.

Reports over the last 30 years about health professionals' knowledge of FASD and how to prevent it have been derived from other countries, especially the USA, Canada and Australia. For example, a postal survey of US obstetricians found that 38% considered an average of one or fewer drinks per day could be consumed safely by pregnant mothers, with 41% considering one to three US standard drinks per day (one standard drink is equivalent to one-and-a-half UK units) acceptable (Abel and Kruger, 1998). In a separate study of 1000 practising US obstetricians, 20% advocated abstinence from alcohol but 13% were unsure what was actually safe. Four per cent of respondents considered that eight or more standard drinks a week did not carry any risk (Diekman, et al., 2000). In a more recent study of US obstetricians 66% of the respondents reported occasional alcohol as unsafe and 45.9% that the effects of alcohol were unclear. Overall, only 78.5% recommend abstinence (Anderson, et al., 2010).

Research from other countries has shown similar findings. Two separate studies from Canada looked at the recommendations regarding safe drinking levels made by midwives and family physicians; 91% recommended abstinence but they considered that not enough information was available to advise others (Tough, et al., 2004). Using a web-based survey, a group of US resident physicians (junior medical doctors) were questioned: 12% of them considered one to three standard drinks per day to be safe; over a quarter felt they had insufficient training but for all but 9% the priority was to protect the foetus from harm (Matthew, et al., 2010). This is not consistent with the legal position in the US and the UK where the rights of the foetus do not take priority over the mother's rights until it is born (Mukherjee, et al. 2007). Matthew and colleagues' study contrasts with findings from a group of Canadian child psychiatrists where 74% of 391 replying to a postal survey focused on managing the mothers' alcohol problems (Tough, Clarke and Hicks, 2003).

Numerous studies have looked at professional groups working with affected individuals. Two early studies from the USA examined the knowledge of paediatricians. A survey of 234 randomly selected paediatricians found that while the majority had heard of FAS (the full syndrome rather than the wider spectrum), they felt unprepared regarding how to manage it and also wished for better education about FASD (Morse, et al., 1992). A later US study of 879 paediatricians from a 3% random sample of those on the US paediatric register found that 62% were confident in being able to identify FAS but only 34% felt then able to manage the disorder (Gahagan, et al., 2006).

Similar findings have been seen elsewhere. A postal study of 1332 paediatricians in Australia indicated that while over 90% reported awareness of already diagnosed cases, only 18.9% felt able to identify the features themselves. Interestingly, 69% of the same group regarded the term FASD as stigmatising (Elliott, et al., 2006), an issue highlighted by other studies. For example, research in South Africa found that alongside poor knowledge and a lack of support services available for FASD, a poor understanding of the children's presentation leading to stigma was evident (Scheepers, 2009).

The above findings suggest a consistent picture across the different countries featuring limited knowledge regarding diagnosis and management as well as stigma associated with the disorder. What UK health professionals know about FASD is currently unclear due to the scarcity of UK-based research in this area. Various questions arise. For example, how confident are professionals at making the diagnosis? Do people in the UK believe the condition is stigmatising and does this affect the levels of diagnosis? How well are professionals able to support and manage women who are pregnant and drinking or those affected by the disorder? What impact does media presentation have on professionals working with people with FASD?

An FASD pilot knowledge questionnaire we conducted on a convenience sample of psychiatrists attending a local academic meeting revealed that they had all heard about FASD but that the majority knew little about it (Mukherjee, Turk and Hollins, 2006). We therefore decided to explore the knowledge and attitudes of UK professionals in more detail.

Methods

To ascertain what is known about FASD in the UK and the impact it has on individuals with the disorder we employed a mixed-methods approach. Three focus groups in different populations were held and supplemented by questionnaires approved by a NHS research ethics committee. Full written consent was obtained from all focus group participants.

Ethical consideration

Permission for the use of unsolicited questionnaires to the general public or direct mail contact was not granted by the research ethics committee. This was due to the potentially sensitive nature of the questions being asked about FASD.

Sample

Recruitment was mandated to be by self-selection only. Advertisements were placed in local hospital departments identified as working with mothers and affected individuals, and letters sent to local GP practices and national professional networks such as the UK perinatal network and the learning disability health network. Those interested were directed to contact the research team. Participants were then invited to research sessions and focus groups. An education workshop was provided for those attending after the research was completed. Up to 10 people were allowed to attend each research session; from those registering to come along to the education session, if above 10, using random number tables, 10 people were randomly selected to participate (Abidin, 1995). All people contacting the team to take part were invited to attend the education session whether or not they had completed the research, which was not mandatory.

Process

Focus groups

Focus groups were conducted on all occasions using semi-structured interviews conducted by the lead researcher (RM). These were allowed to flow freely based on people's responses to initial questions. There was no time limit on the sessions held and participants could express their views openly.

The project research assistant (EW) took field notes and each session was recorded on a digital tape recorder, following written permission from the participants. The transcription was compared to written notes to allow for later data completion and verification. Transcribed and verified data from recordings of the focus group discussions were entered into NVIVO version 8. In order to improve the confirmability and thus the validity of the data, the two researchers (RM and EW) independently conducted their own initial thematic coding before comparing results. Later, joint selective coding of the data to extract themes, as described by Bazeley (2009), was completed.

Questionnaire

Data were collected using a questionnaire consisting of 17 questions developed for this project from prior pilots and wider research findings. Examples included: Have you heard of FASD? Is FASD stigmatising? What level of alcohol exposure is associated with full FAS? Who would you refer to if you saw a child suspected of FASD? (Further questions are highlighted in Tables 2 and 3.)

Questionnaires were completed by those attending focus group and education sessions as well as at professional conferences attended by RM across the UK. An online version of the questionnaire was available for people wishing to complete the questionnaire but unable to attend a session.

Data from questionnaires were entered into SPSS version 18 and frequency data analysed. Comparisons were made between categorical groups and between different demographic backgrounds using chi square tests. Multivariate analysis was not used in this study and no post hoc calculations or corrections were made.

Results

Questionnaire sample

A total of 505 professionals filled in the questionnaire of whom 375 (74%) completed all the questions. Limited comparisons could be made due to sample size and to the level of non-response. Table 1 shows a breakdown of the demographic profiles of all those completing the questionnaires. For example, 83.5 % ($n = 313$) were female, a wide range of ages and

Table 1. Demographic breakdown of participants completing FASD knowledge questionnaires.

	Gender							
	Male				*Female*			
Frequency	62				313			
Valid %	16.5				83.5			
	Age							
	Mean = 44.65				Range = 18–75			
	Grouped age							
	18–29		30–39		40–49		50–59	60+
Frequency	42		68		123		101	27
Valid %	12		19		34		28	7
	Profession							
	GP	Paediatrics	Midwifery	Health visitor	Nurse	Social worker	Mental health	Other
Frequency	62	47	18	13	78	70	20	62
Valid %	17	12	5	3	21	19	5	17
	Number of years in practice							
	Mean = 16.42				Range = 0–45			
	Years in practice							
	0–5 yrs.		6–10 yrs.	11–20 yrs		21–30 yrs	30 + yrs	
Frequency	78		61	93		97	34	
Valid %	21		17	26		27	9	
	Place of work							
	Community			Hospital			Both	
Frequency	281			50			29	
Valid %	78			14			8	
	Regularly treat pregnant women?							
	Yes				No			
Frequency	111				209			
Valid %	35				65			
	Ethnicity							
	White British		White Other		Asian	African Caribbean		Other
Frequency	295		25		30	4		10
Valid %	81		7		8	1		3
	Religion							
	Christian		Muslim	Hindu	Judaism		None	Other
Frequency	214		6	14	2		100	12
Valid %	61		2	4	1		29	3

experience was represented, and 78% worked in the community although the majority of those attending (65%) did not work with pregnant mothers.

Themes

Table 2 examines the responses to the basic questions. Since the numbers in each professional group were too small to draw meaningful conclusions, frequency data alone are presented. Other questions where more detailed knowledge about FASD was sought are shown in Table 3. These data were then considered alongside the focus group themes and five significant ones were identified: lack of knowledge; need for consistent guidance; stigma; need for early intervention; and need for support services.

Lack of knowledge

Data from the questionnaires revealed that 94.2% of the overall participants had heard about FASD, but that they varied in the amount they knew; 72.5% reported that they would like to have more knowledge on the subject. This was also seen in the focus groups: 'I knew very, very little and I still don't really know that much about it.'

This emerged further when more detailed questions were asked. For instance, 72.5% of respondents mentioned that they had insufficient information to give advice to their patients regarding safe alcohol consumption; only 13.7% were able to identify the proportion of the whole FASD spectrum that presented facial features and thus a possible FAS diagnosis

When compared to younger colleagues, older professionals with more experience were more likely to have come across cases of FASD (n = 384 $X^2 = 36.96$ $p < 0.0001$) and also considered it to be a condition that did not improve with age (n = 412 $X^2 = 16.3$ $p = 0.04$).

Need for consistent guidance

When asked to identify government drinking guidance in pregnancy from a list of options, 65.4% correctly recognised the guidance with 58% of them finding it helpful. The impression of inconsistency in the research findings and its subsequent presentation and interpretation led to a widely held perception that no actual position regarding what level of alcohol in pregnancy was safe was correct: 'I think the problem with medical media at the moment is particularly with conflicting advice. People tend to go, "Well, no one knows what they are talking about." '

Of the professionals who claimed to know the government guidance regarding alcohol consumption in pregnancy, a significant proportion did not find this helpful when advising pregnant women (n = 439 $X^2 = 87.12$ $p < 0.0001$) compared to those who found it helpful.

Stigma

Almost 60% of respondents believed that the condition was stigmatising. This was especially true of paediatricians among whom 72% considered that this was so: 'The perception that drinking in pregnancy, in many ways, is more of an underground problem. More stigmatised actually than drug use in pregnancy.'

Table 2. Answers given on structured questionnaire by questions and profession*.

Question		Total	Professional group: GP	Paediatrician	Midwife	Health visitor	Nurse	Social worker	Mental health	Therapist	Other
Have you heard of FASD?	N	419	61	50	18	13	94	79	31	23	50
	Yes	395	55	50	16	12	90	77	29	21	45
	No	24	6	0	2	1	4	2	2	2	5
Is FASD relevant to your specialty?	N	422	62	50	18	13	93	82	32	23	49
	Yes	381	51	49	17	13	83	76	31	21	40
	No	20	5	1	0	0	4	4	1	0	5
	DK	21	6	0	1	0	6	2	0	2	4
Is the term FASD stigmatising?	N	419	62	50	18	11	9	81	32	23	49
	Yes	245	40	36	10	6	55	48	17	11	22
	No	126	19	13	6	2	22	26	11	10	17
	DK	48	3	1	2	3	16	7	4	2	10
Have you been given enough information to advise mothers?	N	378	59	47	18	11	80	70	31	22	40
	Yes	104	26	21	3	4	19	18	4	3	6
	No/DK	274	33	26	15	7	61	52	27	19	34
Affected people with FASD will get better with support. Do you agree?	N	419	60	50	18	12	93	83	31	23	49
	Yes	95	14	7	5	3	26	13	9	9	9
	No	185	28	38	7	3	28	45	12	7	17
	DK	139	18	5	6	6	39	25	10	7	23
What is current pregnancy drinking guidance?	N	390	59	49	16	12	84	78	29	20	43
	Correct	255	34	29	9	10	56	46	27	13	31
	Incorrect	155	25	20	7	2	28	32	2	7	12
Is the drinking guidance helpful in giving safe pregnancy advice?	N	414	60	50	14	13	88	78	26	23	46
	Yes	241	36	26	5	11	53	45	17	12	32
	No	130	16	20	8	2	28	27	8	10	11
	DK	43	8	4	1	0 13	7	6	1	1	3

*N = Number; DK = Don't know.

Table 3. Group totals for further questions on the structured professional questionnaire*.

Question	*Structured answer*	*N*	*%*
What level of alcohol consumption is thought to be associated with full FAS? (Correct, regular, heavy) (N = 498)	1.5/day	43	8.6
	1.5/week	5	1
	Occasional heavy binge	31	6.2
	Regular heavy	167	33.5
	Less than one unit per day	6	1.2
	Level unknown	126	25.3
	Don't know	120	24.1
To whom would you refer if you saw a child suspected with FASD? (N = 454)	Clinical genetics	46	10.1
	Child psychiatry	28	6.2
	Community paediatrician	302	66.5
	Learning disability/psychiatry	25	5.5
	Neurology	26	5.7
	Other	27	5.9

*N = number filling in this question.

Further, the inconsistency of safe drinking messages and the mixed information about the effects of FASD caused some professionals to be uncertain as to the validity of the information they did receive, leading some to dismiss the message as a whole:

> I was talking to a colleague in a young person's addiction service who said, 'Oh, you've got to be aware of those foetal alcohol syndrome groups.' I'm trying to think of the exact word, sort of a maverick's cause. As I say, there is a lot of stuff that's said out there in a very evangelical way of dubious, dubious repute.

Some 10% of those completing the questionnaire, including one midwife, considered FASD to be irrelevant to their specialty.

Need for early intervention

There appeared to be a clear sense that in order to reduce risk, intervention and education about the harms of alcohol needed to be targeted at an early stage. Health interventions needed to be directed at a younger age and leaving it until adulthood was too late: 'They should be giving them information about things like that, shouldn't they? Really about foetal alcohol at an earlier stage. Right from the beginning.'

Need for support services

As shown in Table 3, just over two-thirds (66.5%) regarded community paediatricians as the correct place to refer children with suspected FASD. However, there seemed to be a clear sense that there was no real pathway of support beyond this. The routes to seek help for complicated cases, and the process needed to obtain professional advice and support, seemed to be missing: 'I mean, as professionals, we struggle to find out where to go for support.'

Discussion

Whether it came to giving advice to pregnant mothers or recognising affected individuals, our findings suggest that knowledge about FASD among a wide range of professionals is at best superficial. Many had heard of such disorders but with limited depth to their knowledge. They recognised the message about safe drinking in pregnancy without necessarily knowing the detail or the wider consequences of alcohol for the foetus. This lack of awareness of what to do or how to advise mothers of affected individuals or families makes it difficult for health and social care professions to provide adequate support and is similar to findings from other parts of the world (Anderson, et al., 2010; Diekman, et al., 2000; Elliott, et al., 2006; Gahagan, et al., 2006; Nanson, et al., 1995; Tough, et al., 2005). Our findings go on to suggest that the lack of clarity and confidence have wider implications. Unfortunately the current scientific knowledge base and its reporting seem to have compounded the problem, leading to confusion rather than clarification of what to do for each group.

The importance of recognition

FASD has been described as the most preventable cause of learning difficulties in the world (BMA Board of Science 2007; Mukherjee, Hollins and Turk, 2006). Estimated prevalence rates in studies from many different countries have consistently been shown to be higher than previously thought (BMA Board of Science, 2007; May, et al., 2009; Petkovic and Barisic, 2010).

The condition has potential relevance to a wide range of professionals since it presents with both physical (Autti-Ramo, et al., 2006; Spohr, Willms and Steinhaussen, 1993; Spohr, Willms and Steinhaussen, 1994) and cognitive features (Mattson, et al., 1997; Mattson, et al., 1998; Mattson, et al., 1999; Mattson and Roebuck, 2002; Riley, et al., 2003). As highlighted in our research, professionals considered it important that balanced information was presented when discussing the risks and outcomes of drinking in pregnancy but also that this should be delivered early enough for it to have an impact. Without balance, the perceived evangelical zeal about avoiding alcohol and labelling children with FASD may have led some people to not always believe the message or to see it as relevant to them. In the UK, as in other countries, this remains a challenge (Armstrong, 1998). Further research is required in order to enable professionals to take an educated approach to the disorder, not only to give safe advice during pregnancy but also to recognise and directly manage FASD.

The above findings would suggest that poor knowledge – and perhaps unwillingness or an inability on the part of some professionals to diagnose – may have influenced the perceived stigma and may be one reason for the under-reporting of FASD in the UK (Morleo, et al., 2011).

Consistent messages about safe levels of alcohol in pregnancy and standard methods of diagnosis will need to be adopted if the reliability of these are to improve (Morleo, et al., 2011). Further, our findings suggest that referral pathways – locally, regionally and nationally – need to be better established in order to offer improved and more consistent responses for those diagnosed (also see BMA Board of Science, 2007).

Secondary disabilities

While a great deal of the literature has focused on the level of alcohol that causes harm (Gray, Mukherjee and Rutter, 2009; Kelly, et al. 2010; Sayal, et al. 2007), the outcomes for people and interventional research remain poor (Chandresenna, Mukherjee and Turk, 2009; Streissguth, 1994; Streissguth, et al., 2004; Streissguth and O'Malley, 2000). It is clear that without support for both carers and affected individuals the likelihood of poor outcomes is increased. These include mental health problems for those concerned, as well as effects on society (Barr, et al., 2006; Gray and Mukherjee, 2007; Mukherjee, Hollins and Turk, 2006; Sayal, et al., 2007; Streissguth, 1994). Also, as the relationship between prenatal alcohol exposure and wider neurodevelopmental outcomes becomes clearer (Burd, et al., 2003; Mukherjee, et al., 2011; O'Malley and Storoz, 2003; Oesterheld and Wilson, 1997), the development of pathways to address these issues becomes more important. Our study would suggest that, among professionals, there was a perceived or actual lack of clear referral pathways. This may be part of the reason why people are not diagnosed. Although our research could not prove this conclusively, it may also exacerbate the risk of secondary mental health problems found in other studies. This area warrants further exploration at a service delivery level to ensure that procedures are in place to minimise the long-term impact of FASD.

Support for carers

Professional responsibility goes beyond just the medical model of care. FASD is a condition that requires a broader psychosocial approach. Studies have shown that modification of parenting styles, reducing the stress on the family and good, consistent longer-term structures around the individual are supportive of better and longer-term outcomes (Gelo and O'Malley, 2003; O'Connor, Kogan and Findley, 2002; Streissguth, 1994; Streissguth, et al., 2004). Our study would suggest that the lack of knowledge and, in some, failure to identify FASD as being relevant to their specialty may well preclude this from happening, thus adding to the burden on the individuals and carers affected.

Limitations and conclusions

This piece of research has clear limitations. As one of the first exploratory studies in this area, certain questions may have been leading so that some of the findings require further clarification. Having used a self-selecting group, it does not necessarily reflect the views of broader health practitioners, only those of a subgroup of people who attended. While the sample was random, based on who agreed to complete the questionnaire or attend the meeting, some groups were over-represented and others lacking. For example, the majority of participants were female. People attending conferences may also demonstrate an interest in a particular subject area so that the generalisation of findings may be limited. The lack of involvement of, for instance, obstetricians is a problem and therefore warrants separate study. The restrictions placed by ethical review meant it was not possible to be more selective. One focus group was run with only four people due to failure to attend. Not all the items on the questionnaires were completed, allowing only limited analysis and understanding to be achieved.

Nevertheless, this study offers some initial insight into the current level of knowledge among professionals in the UK. FASD is a condition that presents to many different professional groups. This article suggests the importance of delivering better education for these groups as well as highlighting the need to provide consistent, structured services to help improve the delivery of care to those affected.

Acknowledgement

Many thanks to Jane Hubert for all her help in commenting on the original draft of this article.

References

Abel EL and Kruger M (1998) What do physicians know and say about Fetal Alcohol Syndrome? A survey of obstetricians, paediatricians and family medicine physicians. *Alcoholism Clinical and Experimental Research* 22(9): 51–54.

Abidin R (1995) *Parental Stress Index*, 3rd edn. Florida: PAR Publishing.

Anderson BL, Dang EP, Floyd RL, Sokol R, Mahoney J and Schulkin J (2010) Knowledge, opinions and practice patterns of obstetricians and gynaecologists regarding patients use of alcohol. *Journal of Addiction Medicine* 4(2): 114–121.

Armstrong EM (1998) Diagnosing moral disorder: the discovery and evolution of fetal alcohol syndrome. *Social Science & Medicine* 47(12): 2025–2042.

Autti-Ramo I, Fagerlaud A, Ervalhatri N, Loimu L, Korkman M and Hoyme HE (2006) Fetal alcohol spectrum disorders in Finland. *American Journal of Clinical Genetics* 140: 137–143.

Barr H, Bookstein FL, O'Malley K, Connor PD, Huggins JE and Streissguth AP (2006) Binge drinking during pregnancy as a predictor of psychiatric disorders on the structured clinical interview for DSM-IV in young adult offspring. *American Journal of Psychiatry* 163: 1061–1065.

Bazeley P (2009) *Qualitative Data Analysis with NVIVO*. London: Sage.

BMA Board of Science (2007) *Fetal Alcohol Spectrum Disorders: A guide for healthcare practitioners*. London: BMA Publishing.

Burd L, Klug MG, Martsolf JT and Kerbeshian J (2003) Fetal alcohol syndrome: neuropsychiatric phenomics. *Neurotoxicology and Teratology* 25(6): 697–705.

Chandresenna A, Mukherjee RAS and Turk JT (2009) Fetal alcohol spectrum disorders: an overview of interventions for affected individuals. *Child and Adolescent Mental Health* 14(4): 162–169.

Diekman ST, Floyd RL, Decoufle P, Schulkin J, Ebrahim SH and Sokol R (2000) A survey of obstetricians and gynaecologists on their patients' alcohol use during pregnancy. *Obstetrics & Gynecology* 95(5): 756–763.

Elliott E, Payne J, Haan E and Bower C (2006) Diagnosis of Fetal Alcohol Syndrome and alcohol use in pregnancy: a survey of paediatricians' knowledge, attitudes and practice. *Journal of Paediatrics and Child Health* 42(11): 698–703.

Gahagan S, Sharpe TT, Brimacombe M, Fry Johnson Y, Levine R, Mengel M, O'Connor M, Paley B, Adubato S and Brenneman G (2006) Knowledge, training and experience in the care of children with FAS. *Paediatrics* 118(3): 657–668.

Gelo J and O'Malley K (2003) Family stress in parenting a child or adolescent with FASD. *Iceberg* 13(1): 1–4.

Gray R and Mukherjee RAS (2007) A psychiatrists' guide to fetal alcohol spectrum disorders in mothers who drank heavily during pregnancy. *Advances in Mental Health and Intellectual Disability* 1(3): 19–26.

Gray R, Mukherjee RAS and Rutter M (2009) Alcohol consumption during pregnancy and its effects on neurodevelopment: what is known and what remains uncertain. *Addiction* 104: 1270–1273.

Kelly YJ, Sacker A, Gray R, Kelly J, Wolke D, Jead J and Quigley MA (2010) Light drinking during pregnancy: still no increased risk for socioemotional difficulties or cognitive deficits at 5 years of age. *Journal of Epidemiology and Community Health* 66(1): 41–8.

Matthew AK, Bruce C, Sharpe R and Littner Y (2010) Can we improve the advice we give to women about prenatal alcohol exposure? *Alcoholism: Clinical & Experimental Research* 34(6): 210.

Mattson SN and Roebuck TM (2002) Acquisition and retention of verbal and nonverbal information in children with heavy prenatal alcohol exposure. *Alcoholism: Clinical & Experimental Research* 26(6): 875–882.

Mattson SN, Goodman AM, Caine C, Delis D and Riley EP (1999) Executive functioning in children with heavy prenatal alcohol exposure. *Alcoholism: Clinical & Experimental Research* 23(11): 1808–1815.

Mattson SN, Riley EP, Gramling L, Delis D and Jones KL (1997) Heavy prenatal alcohol exposure with or without physical features of fetal alcohol syndrome leads to IQ deficits. *Journal of Pediatrics* 131(5): 718–721.

Mattson SN, Riley EP, Gramling L, Delis D and Jones KL (1998) Neuropsychological comparison of alcohol exposed children with or without physical features of fetal alcohol syndrome. *Neuropsychology* 12(1): 146–153.

May PA, Gossage JP, Kalberg WO, Robinson LK, Buckley D, Manning M and Hoyme HE (2009) Prevalence and epidemiological characteristics of FASD from various research methods with an emphasis on in-school studies. *Developmental Disabilites Research Reviews* 15: 176–192.

Morleo M, Woolfall K, Dedman D, Mukherjee RAS, Bellis MA and Cook PA (2011) Under-reporting of Fetal Alcohol Spectrum Disorders: an analysis of Hospital Episode Statistics. *BMC Paediatrics* 14(11): 1–6.

Morse BA, Idelson RK, Sachs WH, Weiner L and Kaplan LC (1992) Paediatricians' perspective on FAS. *Substance Abuse* 4(2): 187–195.

Mukherjee RAS, Hollins S and Turk J (2006) Fetal Alcohol Spectrum Disorder: an overview. *Journal of the Royal Society of Medicine* 99(6): 298–302.

Mukherjee RAS, Turk J and Hollins S (2006) Psychiatric comorbidity in fetal alcohol syndrome. *Psychiatric Bulletin* 30: 194–195.

Mukherjee RAS, Eastman N, Turk J and Hollins S (2007) Fetal Alcohol Syndrome: law and ethics. *The Lancet* 369: 1149–1150.

Mukherjee RAS, Layton M, Yacoub E and Turk JT (2011) Autism and autistic traits in people exposed to heavy prenatal alcohol: data from a clinical series of 21 individuals and a nested case control study. *Advances in Mental Health and Learning Disability* 5: 43–49.

Nanson JL, Bolaria R, Snyder RE, Morse BA and Weiner L (1995) Physicians' awareness of FAS. *Journal of the Canadian Medical Association* 152(7): 1071–1076.

O'Connor MJ, Kogan N and Findley R (2002) Prenatal alcohol exposure and attachment behaviour in children. *Alcoholism: Clinical & Experimental Research* 26(10): 1592–1602.

O'Malley KD and Storoz L (2003) Fetal alcohol spectrum disorder and ADHD: diagnostic implications and therapeutic consequences. *Expert Review of Neurotherapeutics* 3(4): 477–489.

Oesterheld JR and Wilson A (1997) ADHD and FAS. *Journal of the American Academy of Child & Adolescent Psychiatry* 36(9): 1163.

Petkovic G and Barisic I (2010) FAS prevalence in a sample of urban schoolchildren in Croatia. *Reproductive Toxicology* 29: 237–241.

Riley EP, Mattson SN, Li TK, Jacobson SW, Coles CD, Kodituwakku PW, Adams CM and Korkman MI (2003) Neurobehavioral consequences of prenatal alcohol exposure: an international perspective. *Alcoholism: Clinical & Experimental Research* 27(2): 362–73.

Sayal K, Heron J, Golding J and Emond A (2007) Prenatal alcohol exposure and gender differences in childhood mental health problems: a longitudinal population based study. *Paediatrics* 119: 426–434.

Scheepers P (2009) *Educators' Knowledge and Attitudes Towards FASD.* Unpublished thesis. Stellenbosch University, South Africa. Available at: http://scholar.sun.ac.za/handle/10019.1/2079.

Spohr HL, Willms J and Steinhaussen HC (1993) Prenatal alcohol exposure and long-term developmental consequences. *The Lancet* 341: 907–910.

Spohr HL, Willms J and Steinhaussen HC (1994) The fetal alcohol syndrome in adolescence. *Acta Paediatrics* 404: 19–26.

Streissguth AP (1994) A long term perspective of FAS. *Alcohol Health & Research World* 18(1): 74–81.

Streissguth AP, Bookstein FL, Barr HM, Sampson PD, O'Malley KD and Kogan Young J (2004) Risk factors for adverse life outcomes in fetal alcohol syndrome and fetal alcohol effects. *Developmental and Behavioural Pediatrics* 25(4): 228–238.

Streissguth AP and O'Malley K (2000) Neuropsychiatric implications and long-term consequences of fetal alcohol spectrum disorders. *Seminars in Clinical Neuropsychiatry* 5(3): 177–90.

Tough SC, Clarke M and Hicks M (2003) Knowledge and attitudes of Canadian psychiatrists regarding FASD. *Canadian Journal of Child and Adolescent Psychiatry* 12(3): 64–71.

Tough SC, Clarke M, Hicks M and Clarren S (2004) Clinical practice characteristics and preconception counseling strategies of health care providers who recommend alcohol abstinence during pregnancy. *Alcoholism: Clinical and Experimental Research* 28(11): 1724–1731.

Tough SC, Clarke M, Hicks M and Clarren S (2005) Variation in health care provider definitions of moderate consumption during pregnancy: results from a Canadian survey. *Therapeutic Drug Monitoring* 27(3): 290–296.

Dr Raja Mukherjee is a Consultant Psychiatrist, Specialist FASD Behavioural Clinic, NHS Surrey and Borders Partnership, UK.

Elizabeth Wray is a Research Assistant to Dr Mukherjee.

Leopold Curfs is Professor of Learning Disabilities at Maastricht University Medical Centre, Department of Clinical Genetics, and Director of the Governor Kremers Centre at the Academic Hospital, Maastricht and Maastricht University, Netherlands.

Baroness Sheila Hollins is Emeritus Professor of Psychiatry of Learning Disability at St George's University of London, and Chair of the BMA Board of Science, UK.

Article

Adoption & Fostering
2015, Vol. 39(3) 225–234

DOI: 10.1177/0308575915594985
adoptionfostering.sagepub.com

Identifying children who are at risk of FASD in Peterborough: working in a community clinic without access to gold standard diagnosis

Geraldine Gregory
Cambridgeshire and Peterborough NHS Foundation Trust, UK

Venkat Reddy
Peterborough Integrated Child Health Services, UK

Clare Young
Peterborough City Council, UK

Abstract

The number of UK children seen with complex behaviour difficulties where there is a history of exposure to alcohol and/or drugs prenatally appears to be increasing at an alarming rate. Community paediatricians work with vulnerable children and also act as medical advisers to adoption panels, so they have a unique overview of the unmet needs of looked after children affected by Foetal Alcohol Spectrum Disorders (FASD). This article reports on two simple audits of children seen in a community paediatric clinic setting. The first audit counted the number of children seen during a period of two-and-a-half years between April 2010 and August 2013, where there was a clear prenatal history of alcohol exposure. This audit also specifically looked at how many of these children might have Foetal Alcohol Syndrome (FAS) or FASD. Seventy-two children were given such a diagnosis within the time frame. The second audit reported on children looked after and children put forward for adoption during a 12-month period from January 2013 to December 2013. It reported a history of prenatal exposure in 55 out of 160 health assessments for looked after children (34%) and in 34 out of 45 medicals for adoption (75%).

Keywords

FAS, FASD, community paediatrician, looked after children, audits, Peterborough

Corresponding author:
Geraldine Gregory, Peterborough Integrated Child Health Services, Cambridgeshire and Peterborough NHS Foundation Trust, 80 Thorpe Road, Peterborough PE3 6AP, UK.
Email: ges.gregory@cpft.nhs.uk

Background

In recent years the number of children seen with complex behaviour difficulties where there is a history of exposure to alcohol and/or drugs prenatally seems to be rising at an alarming rate. The prevalence of Foetal Alcohol Spectrum Disorders (FASD) in the UK population is unknown but estimates for Canada and the USA suggest rates as high as 1:100, with the prevalence of Foetal Alcohol Syndrome (FAS) at 1:1000 (BMA Board of Science, 2007; Chudley, et al., 2005; May and Gossage, 2001). Looked after children (LAC) are a particularly vulnerable group for whom the likelihood of prenatal alcohol and substance exposure is greater than for the general population. Those with FASD should be identified early so that an accurate assessment, appropriate support and advice for carers, early intervention for challenging behaviours and support for learning difficulties can be offered.

When FASD are suspected, the community paediatric department is often the first place that a referral for assessment is sent. There is little evidence in the UK that these departments have a clear understanding of the magnitude of the problem or the ability to assess and manage the rapidly increasing numbers of affected children (Elliott, et al., 2006; Eustace, Kang and Coombs, 2003; Mukherjee, Hollins and Turk, 2006a). There are no FASD prevalence studies in the UK and so doctors are unable to inform the health commissioners of the services needed to provide an adequate level of care. Until we start to recognise FASD and collect prevalence data this situation will not change.

Community paediatricians work with vulnerable children, including those looked after, and also act as medical advisers to adoption panels. Therefore they have a unique overview of the unmet needs of children at risk in their locality (Gahagan, et al., 2006). This article reports on two simple audits of children seen in a community paediatric clinic in the UK city of Peterborough. The first audit counted the number seen during a period of two-and-a-half years between April 2010 and August 2013, where there was a clear prenatal history of alcohol exposure. This audit also specifically looked at how many of these children might have FAS/FASD. The second audit reported on children looked after and children put forward for adoption during a 12-month period from January 2013 to December 2013.

Peterborough, in the east of England, has a high level of social deprivation; it also has seen a large increase in population in the last few years. According to demographic data gathered by the Peterborough Children's Trust Partnership Board (2010), the rates for childhood poverty were significantly higher than the rest of the UK: in eight of the 24 local authority districts, the poverty rate was over 30%, with the highest reported at 35%. The average rate for the UK was 21.4%.

Peterborough City Council statistics for 2012 record a population of 186,400. There were 3300 live births per year, 14,700 children under five and 34,600 children aged 5–19. Since 2004, there has been a large increase in the number of migrants, particularly from Eastern Europe, and the population has risen by 12.3%.

Before the audit started in 2010, only two children diagnosed with FAS were recorded on the community child health system and none with FASD. Documentation of possible pre-birth exposure to alcohol and drugs was patchy and rarely linked to the presenting problem for the child. Some clinicians were more likely to record this information than others; in many cases, despite the information being available, it was not documented at all in the child's records. Professionals from all disciplines referring children for assessment provided inconsistent information on substance misuse in birth mothers and when mentioned, it was often part of a picture of domestic violence rather than specifically around any prenatal exposure experienced by a child.

The gold standard for making a diagnosis of FAS/FASD

The gold standard for assessments leading to diagnosis in the USA and Canada (Astley, 2004; Chudley, et al., 2005) always involves a multidisciplinary team. This is because there is no one test for FASD. Such a team would include a paediatrician, one or two psychologists, a speech and language therapist, an occupational therapist, a social worker and a family advocate. Before clinical assessment, time is taken to review a child's clinical records and collect pertinent background information. The clinical assessment is then carried out over several hours, after which a comprehensive report with diagnostic information, advice and recommendations is made. A feedback session for carers and professionals is also offered.

Like most community paediatric departments in the UK, resources and staff are limited and access to this level of multiagency assessment is simply not available. It was therefore impossible for the department to replicate this standard of assessment.

For the purpose of the audits a diagnosis of FAS was made using the standard US and Canadian criteria (Chudley, et al., 2005):

- *growth deficiency before and after birth* – weight and length/height below the 10th centiles;[1]
- *FAS facial phenotype* – short palpebral fissure length (distance between the inner and outer canthus of the eye), smooth or flat philtrum and thin upper lip as ranked on a lip-philtrum guide;
- *central nervous system structural/functional abnormalities in three or more domains* – this includes microcephaly, neurological signs, deficits in cognition, academic achievement, executive functioning and poor working memory, and difficulties in social communication, abstract reasoning, adaptive behaviour and attention deficits;
- *a confirmed history of prenatal alcohol exposure.*

FASD was diagnosed if the child did not have all the facial features and/or growth was not affected, but did meet the other criteria. Assessments for cognitive functioning were not available for every child and executive function testing was hardly ever an option. Central nervous system functional abnormalities were therefore assessed on clinical assessment using standard developmental assessment tools or if there was evidence of attention deficit. Occupational therapy assessments were available, but speech and language assessments were not. The audit method required an identified problem in three or more areas of cognitive functioning to make a diagnosis.

Assessments for children thought to have FASD are often requested in a piecemeal fashion, with paediatricians asking for sequential assessments with little opportunity for joined-up thinking between the different professional groups. Not surprisingly, the process took a long time and it was very difficult for children's carers to understand the process and when and how a diagnosis could be made.

Audit I

This retrospective audit was carried out on children who had been seen in the city's community paediatric clinics between April 2010 and August 2013. In all cases, the children had been referred for an assessment of complex behavioural difficulties. Also included were looked after children who had been referred for statutory health assessments where behavioural difficulties were noted at the time they were seen. In most cases, the information on prenatal alcohol and/or drug exposure came to light only during the assessment, though in a few cases the information was provided as part of the request for assessment. Simultaneously, to increase local knowledge and awareness of FAS/FASD there was a programme of intensive training for local multiagency groups, including health professionals, social workers, teachers, drug and alcohol teams, foster carers and prospective adopters. It was clear that towards the end of this audit, when some index cases had been identified with FAS/FASD, their siblings or similar cases known to professionals were more likely to be referred directly for assessment and advice.

Seventy-two children were identified as fulfilling the diagnostic criteria for having FAS or FASD (Table 1). Before the audit, there were only two cases on Peterborough's community child health system.

Forty-three of the children (60%) were looked after by the local authority; 14 were adopted and of these, six were given a diagnosis before the adoption order was made. In eight cases the diagnosis was made after adoption, when the child was presenting with difficulties. In most of the latter group the adoptive parents had no prior knowledge of possible long-term problems. For adopted children there is an emotional impact from being diagnosed with FAS/FASD many years after adoption. For parents it was usually a relief to know 'what was wrong' with their child as they were often given numerous conflicting explanations for their child's difficulties. However, the realisation that they had adopted a child who was likely to have continuing long-term needs was very hard for most parents to come to terms with, especially when they looked at the impact on their whole family.

Fifteen children were seen who were neither in the care of the local authority nor adopted but living with their birth families. Three resided with their maternal grandmothers, five with birth fathers, four with birth mothers, two with an aunt and one with a maternal cousin. These families did not have the assistance of children's services or adoption agencies and

Table 1. Number of children identified as having a diagnosis of FAS/FASD between April 2010 and August 2013.

	Looked after children	*Adopted children*	*Children living in birth families*	*Total*
Total number diagnosed with FAS/FASD	43	14	15	72
FAS	12	5	8	25
FASD	31	9	7	47
Male	24	9	10	43
Female	19	5	5	29
Age 0–4 years	10	5	7	22
Age 5–10 years	16	6	6	28
Age 11–16 years	13	3	2	18
Age 16+	4	0	0	4

often struggled to receive adequate understanding and support. In four cases, the children continued to live with their birth mothers who still had their own issues with drug and alcohol use. For all these children it was not easy to pick out specific alcohol-related neurodevelopmental difficulties. This was due to other complications, a fluctuating level of care, inadequate behavioural management and unresolved attachment issues, or in many cases a combination of all these factors. Nevertheless, it is important to recognise that the children themselves had intrinsic and specific neurodevelopmental difficulties due to alcohol induced brain damage as well as to the detrimental environments in which they were growing up.

The audit also identified another group of 25 children with a known diagnosis of Neonatal Abstinence Syndrome (NAS) after birth, who presented with difficult or challenging behaviours in later life (Table 2). For 10 of the 25 (40%) with a history of NAS there was enough evidence for a diagnosis of FAS/FASD to be made, although alcohol in pregnancy does not produce a recognised withdrawal syndrome in the neonatal period. This audit would suggest that a significant number of drug dependent mothers also misuse alcohol.

At risk but no diagnosis

The audit also identified a number of children who had evidence of exposure to drugs and/or alcohol in the prenatal period, but who did not display significant challenging behaviours or learning difficulties and who were seen in the community clinics for other reasons or for statutory health assessments. Twenty-four of these children (57%) were adopted (Table 3). Often they had some behavioural difficulty but there was insufficient evidence to make a diagnosis of FASD. These children were considered to be at risk of but not showing evidence of such a disorder at the time they were seen.

Of the adopted children, nine had a history of NAS treated after birth but at the time they were seen were not presenting with any other problems. An additional nine had a clear history of drug use in pregnancy but were not clinically treated for NAS after birth.

Thirty-two children (76%) were still under the age of four. However, they may develop problems in later life as FAS/FASD often present for the first time in primary school, at transition to secondary school or even at school leaving age.

Table 2. Children identified during the audit period April 2010 to August 2013 as having a history of Neonatal Abstinence Syndrome (NAS).

	Looked after children	*Adopted children*	*Children living with birth families*	*Total*
NAS	11	10	4	25
Male	3	5	3	11
Female	8	5	1	14
Age 0–4 years	9	9	1	19
Age 5–10 years	2	1	3	6
Age 11–16 years	0	0	0	0
Age over 16 years	0	0	0	0

Table 3. At risk: children who had documentation of exposure to drugs and/or alcohol in the prenatal period but were not presenting with challenging behaviours.

Total	*42*
Male	21
Female	21
Age 0–4	32
5–10	9
11+	1
In care	13
Adopted	24
Living with mother	3
Living with aunt	1
Living with maternal grandmother	1

Overall findings

This first audit was a retrospective assessment of how many children were noted to have a history of prenatal alcohol and drug exposure and to see how many were diagnosed with FAS/FASD. As it was a retrospective study, it would be difficult to give this number as an exact percentage of the total numbers of children assessed in the department. However, as an approximation, the community paediatric department received 2049 new referrals and 158 referrals for initial health assessment for children taken into care. Three per cent of all those seen had a diagnosis of FAS/FASD and for the looked after children it was 27% (43 cases out of the 158).

The number of children identified as being at risk increased steadily during the course of the audit. It is relevant that it also took place alongside an intensive training programme across a range of different agencies about the risks of drug and alcohol use in pregnancy. At the end of the audit period, most health professionals and social workers had changed their approach and were actively seeking information on prenatal alcohol and drug use as part of their initial assessments.

As this audit had found very high levels of affected children in the looked after and adopted populations, a second audit of looked after children (LAC) health assessments and adoption medical assessments was carried out for a 12-month period between January and December in 2013. The aim was to count the number of children seen where there was a clear history of prenatal alcohol and/or drug exposure documented in the prenatal period and measure this as a percentage of the total number of children assessed.

Audit 2

The second audit looked at initial and review health assessments carried out by community paediatricians during the 12 months. If a child was seen more than once during 2013, the case was only counted once and information on exposure to alcohol and drugs was only

Table 4. Conditions identified in children seen for LAC health assessments in 2013.*

Total number of health assessments carried out in January–December 2013	*160*
Drugs and/or alcohol abuse is a significant factor, including all children with NAS, FAS and FASD	55 (34%)
Developmental delay	28 (17.5%)
Exposure to significant domestic violence	17 (10%)
Child sexual abuse	14
Autism and ASD	14
Significant neglect	11
Parental mental illness	10
ADHD	7
Identified chromosome disorder	5
Challenging behaviours – not otherwise classified	3
Emotional abuse	2
Foetal Valproate Syndrome	1
Prematurity 27 weeks, oxygen dependent for 12 months	1
Cleft palate with syndrome	2
Cerebral palsy	2
Hemiplegia	2
Epidermolysis bullosa	1
Cystic fibrosis	1
Tic disorder	1
ME (chronic fatigue syndrome)	1
Myotonia syndrome with developmental delay	1
Parent in prison (taken into custody after the assessment)	1

*Note: Some of the children seen had more than one identified problem and some had none, hence the number of conditions listed does not equal the number of assessments carried out.

recorded as one event. Children and young people seen for health assessments by the specialist nurses mostly involved uncomplicated review visits and they were not counted.
A total of 160 assessments were recorded in the year. Of these, 88 were initial assessments for children who had recently come into care and 72 were review assessments seen by a paediatrician, as they were noted to have complex needs. The age range of the majority of children was between birth and 16 years, with just three young people over 16.

A summary of the main clinical health needs and any neurodevelopmental difficulty was documented for each child. Risk factors such as significant maternal health illness were noted as well as child abuse, if it was deemed to be significantly contributing to the child's behaviour. A record was made where it was known that maternal drug and alcohol use was a significant factor in the prenatal period. When it came to older children, it was often difficult to find the evidence of prenatal exposure in the clinical records.

Results

In most cases the children had more than one significant factor. Table 4 lists the health concerns for the 160 children seen.

It was noted that for 55 (34%) alcohol and/or drug use was noted to be a significant factor that needed to be considered as part of the ongoing assessment for the child. In 2013, this was by far the most significant health concern for children looked after and dwarfed all other health needs. All these children need long-term specialist follow-up, a situation which is neither available nor resourced at present.

Adoption reports

All adoption reports prepared and written in 2013 were audited, 45 of them specifically for the purpose of adoption. Some of these children also would have been seen as looked after children and so counted in the group above.

Among the 45 reports, 34 children (75%) had a positive history of exposure to alcohol and/or drugs in the prenatal period. While the number of reports written is not high, all of these children were under the age of five years, with the majority under two. Clinical symptoms often are not present at such a young age and physical characteristics may not be evident.

Consideration must be given to what advice and information is given to potential adopters and adoptive parents need access to assessment and long-term support, if appropriate at any time in the future. This finding is especially relevant to adopters proposing to adopt young children or babies, since few of them will have developed problems at the time of being placed (Autti-Rämö, 2002; Mukherjee, Hollins and Turk, 2006b; Mukherjee, et al., 2013; O'Leary, 2004; Riley and McGee, 2005; Sood, et al., 2001).

Conclusions

This article reports the findings of two community audits that identified children with documented prenatal exposure to alcohol with or without drugs.

During the timespan of the first audit, 72 children were given a diagnosis of FAS/FASD based on the best clinical evidence available at the time. Before, there had been only two recognised cases of FAS and no cases of FASD recorded in the community child health system. This is equivalent to about 3% of all referrals and 27% of referrals for looked after children.

The second audit revealed that 34% of children coming into care, 75% of whom were being put forward for adoption, had prenatal alcohol exposure. These are children at high risk of neurodevelopmental disorders and FASD.

Access to cognitive, behavioural and executive functioning assessments plays a key part in making a diagnosis of FAS and FASD, yet these are not widely available to most community paediatricians working with vulnerable children. It might be suggested that not being able to match the criteria for a 'gold standard' assessment partly could be to blame for the under-reporting of cases and lack of interest shown by other health agencies.

Vulnerable children presenting with difficult and challenging behaviours are likely to have more than one problem. There is a high rate of other developmental disorders such as attention deficit hyperactivity disorders (ADHD) and autistic spectrum disorders (O'Leary, 2004; Riley and McGee, 2005; Welch-Carre, 2005). Attachment disorders are also likely to be a significant factor. Whereas previously many challenging behaviours or disrupted placements have been put down to attachment alone, it is now becoming apparent that children may well have undiagnosed FASD.

This small audit revealed that around 40% of babies with symptoms of neonatal drug withdrawal also had evidence of FASD. More work needs to be done nationally to follow up these children, so that appropriate pathways of care can be set up. Many of the young babies with NAS are being adopted and potential adopters need to be given the correct information and advice at the outset of placement to ensure they are able to meet the child's needs. A number of infants with NAS are discharged home with their birth mothers who are on drug programmes. These children must be identified as being more likely to have additional needs and it should be recognised that emerging behavioural problems cannot simply be attributed to the level of parenting, and appropriate assessment for neurodevelopmental difficulties needs to be offered.

Since the audits, changes to how children are assessed have been made locally and the training programme has continued to raise awareness. This has resulted in more children being referred for assessment and the information regarding prenatal exposure to alcohol, drugs and other substances being requested at a much earlier point prior to referral.

The most obvious difficulty in trying to persuade health commissioners of the need to fund services for assessments and management of cases of FAS/FASD is the lack of clarity regarding the number of children affected. It has wrongly been assumed that this is a rare disorder and that no additional support is needed to manage them. This is the first time that the workload which this population of children is generating, both now and in the future, has been documented. Our audits clearly show that exposure to alcohol and drugs in the prenatal period is one of the biggest issues facing health and social care. The UK urgently needs a statistically accurate prospective prevalence study to plan clinical services for the future for the nation's most vulnerable children.

Note

1. Centile charts show the position of a measured parameter within a statistical distribution. They do not show if that parameter is normal or abnormal but how it compares with that measurement in other individuals. For example, if a parameter such as height is on the 3rd centile, this means that for every 100 children of that age, 3 would be expected to be shorter and 97 taller. On the 97th centile, 97 would be shorter and 3 taller.

References

Astley SJ (2004) *Diagnostic Guide for Fetal Alcohol Spectrum Disorders: The 4-digit diagnostic code.* 3rd edn. Seattle, WA: University of Washington Publication Services.

Autti-Rämö I (2002) Fetal alcohol syndrome – a multifaceted condition. *Developmental Medicine and Child Neurology* 44(2): 141–144.

BMA Board of Science (2007) *Foetal Alcohol Spectrum Disorders: A guide for health professionals.* Available at: www.nofas.uk.org/PDF/BMA%20REPORT%204%20JUNE%202007.pdf.

Chudley AE, Conroy J, Cook JL, et al. (2005) Foetal Alcohol Spectrum Disorder: Canadian guidelines for diagnosis. *Canadian Medical Association Journal* 172(5): s1–s21.

Elliott EJ, Payne J, Haan E and Bower C (2006) Diagnosis of fetal alcohol syndrome and alcohol use in pregnancy: a survey of paediatricians' knowledge, attitudes and practice. *Journal of Paediatrics and Child Health* 42(11): 698–703.

Eustace LW, Kang DH and Coombs D (2003) Fetal alcohol syndrome: a growing concern for health care professionals. *Journal of Obstetric, Gynecologic and Neonatal Nursing* 32(2): 215–221.

Gahagan S, Sharpe TT, Brimacombe M, et al. (2006) Paediatricians' knowledge, training, and experience in the care of children with fetal alcohol syndrome. *Pediatrics* 118(3). doi: 10.1542/peds.2005-0516.

May PA and Gossage JP (2001) Estimating the prevalence of foetal alcohol syndrome: a summary. *Alcohol and Health Research* 25(3): 159–167.

Mukherjee RAS, Hollins S and Turk J (2006a) Foetal alcohol spectrum disorder: an overview. *Journal of the Royal Society of Medicine* 99(6): 298–302.

Mukherjee RAS, Hollins S and Turk J (2006b) Psychiatric comorbidity in foetal alcohol syndrome. *Psychiatric Bulletin* 30: 194–195. doi: 10.1192/pb.30.5.194-c.

Mukherjee RAS, Wray E, Commers M, Hollins S and Curfs L (2013) The impact of raising a child with FASD upon carers: findings from a mixed methodology study in the UK. *Adoption & Fostering* 37(1): 43–56.

O'Leary CM (2004) Foetal alcohol syndrome: diagnosis, epidemiology, and developmental outcomes. *Journal of Paediatrics and Child Health* 40(1–2): 2–7.

Peterborough Children's Trust Partnership Board (2010) *Children and Young People's Needs Assessment. Section 1: Demographics and contextual information.* Available at: childrenandfamilies-cypp-needsassessment-demographics.pdf.

Riley EP and McGee CL (2005) Fetal alcohol spectrum disorders: an overview with emphasis on changes in brain and behaviour. *Experimental Biology and Medicine* 230: 357–365.

Sood B, Delaney-Black V, Covington C, et al. (2001) Prenatal alcohol exposure and childhood behaviour at age 6 to 7 years: I. dose-response effect. *Pediatrics* 108: e34.

Welch-Carre E (2005) The neurodevelopmental consequences of prenatal alcohol exposure. *Advances in Neonatal Care* 5(4): 217–229.

Dr Geraldine Gregory is a Consultant Community Paediatrician, Peterborough Integrated Child Health Services, Cambridgeshire and Peterborough NHS Foundation Trust, Peterborough, UK.

Dr Venkat Reddy is Lead Clinician, Community Paediatrics and Child Health, Peterborough Integrated Child Health Services, Peterborough, UK.

Dr Clare Young is Lead Clinical Psychologist, Fostering and Adoption Psychology Services, Peterborough City Council, Peterborough, UK.

Article

Adoption & Fostering
2015, Vol. 39(3) 235–246

DOI: 10.1177/0308575915595197
adoptionfostering.sagepub.com

'I know that I'm in my own world; it's OK, they know me here': the challenge of coping with FASD in educational settings

Brian Roberts
Independent trainer and consultant, UK

Abstract
In July 2012, the UK's All Party Parliamentary Group published their long-awaited report into the educational attainment of looked after children. This report included 10 key recommendations to improve practice. One was that 'teachers should receive greater training to improve their understanding of and ability to manage issues such as trauma, attachment and Foetal Alcohol Spectrum Disorders (FASD)'. Members of the working group understood that these conditions can have significant and lifelong effects on the education and life chances of children who have been in care. It could be argued that of the three conditions listed, FASD may well be the most significant but is often the most overlooked and misunderstood. FASD can place a significant barrier to learning, but currently is so poorly understood that teachers and schools struggle to provide the best learning environments.

Keywords
FASD, education, children in care

Introduction

After teaching in secondary schools for over 10 years, I became a foster carer providing a permanent home for sibling groups. It was only then that I realised how little I knew and how poorly I had been prepared to meet the needs of vulnerable students in my classroom. That was over 20 years ago. I am still a foster carer and it has changed my professional career. This article tells part of that story.

Corresponding author:
Brian Roberts, Field of Enterprise Training and Consultancy, 18 Doddington Road, Chatteris, Cambridgeshire PE16 6UA, UK.
Email: fieldofenterprise@gmail.com

Eleven years ago, a sibling group of three girls was placed with us; subsequently they secured a permanent home when we took out special guardianship orders for them. Our experience with these girls challenged everything that my wife and I had learned in fostering and in our professional careers. I was an experienced secondary school teacher and my wife had been an officer in charge of a residential children's home. Nothing we tried had the desired or expected effect. Of course, we know now that all three girls were affected by FASD to varying degrees.

For the last seven years I have been a virtual head[1] for looked after children in two English local authorities. During this time it has become abundantly clear that the incidence of FASD in the cohort of children with care experience is far higher than was reported a decade ago. I believe that FASD is making a significant but unrecognised contribution to our ability to close the educational attainment gap between looked after children and their peers. As my wife and I continue to foster, the majority of the babies and toddlers we provide a home for appear to be affected by the same condition.

The costs of closing the achievement gap

All four countries in the UK have made raising the educational attainment of looked after children a key priority. However, closing the gap between their achievement in school and that of their peers who have never been in care has not been realised (e.g. Jackson, 2014). In England, considerable time and effort have been expended by thousands of people to this end and millions of pounds have been spent. In the financial year 2013–14, just over £38 million was spent on the Pupil Premium[2] alone for looked after children (Department for Education, 2013). In 2014–15, Pupil Premium Plus changed the criteria from having been looked after for six months to having been looked after for one day, and it includes children who have achieved permanence through adoption and special guardianship orders. The funding allocated is close to £100 million (Department for Education, 2014).

These sums are only a portion of the total expenditure on looked after children, as yet more is spent in schools and by local authorities to support educational achievement. Despite this, the gap has not closed as fast as anticipated. It now seems increasingly likely that unrecognised FASD could contribute to the reasons why expenditure has failed to produce the proportionate and desired effects.

There is no such research in the UK, but worldwide studies suggest a prevalence of 1:1000 children with Foetal Alcohol Syndrome (FAS) and 1:100 with FASD. This means there are at least three to four affected pupils in the average UK primary school and at least 10 to 20 children in each secondary one. In a local rural primary school with a school roll of just under 400, there were five identified, affected pupils in 2013–14, all of them with a care experience.[3] However, there were also several other pupils in the school who displayed very similar behaviours and learning problems. These children were neither formally identified nor known to social care agencies. This is an increasingly common situation with teachers identifying behaviours suggesting prenatal exposure to alcohol in more children than those formally diagnosed.

FASD can affect any child whose mother drank alcohol while pregnant. However, the effects on the education of affected children who have experience of the care system, whether they are still looked after, have secured permanence or have returned to live with birth relatives, are complex and worrying. From my own experience, plus various discussions with professionals working with looked after children in English local authorities, the incidence of FASD in children with a care background seems to be far higher than in the population as a whole, with current unvalidated figures suggesting rates of between 30% and 90% being affected to some degree.

The barriers that FASD places on the ability to learn

The impact that FASD has on a child's ability to learn is poorly understood, even by many people closely linked to their education. From the outset, it must be acknowledged that those affected are some of the most difficult and challenging students to have in any classroom. This is illustrated by the following three examples from the last two years:

(1) At the beginning of Year 11, a 15-year-old boy took a knife into his secondary school. He had picked up the knife when carpets were being fitted in his home and liked it so much that he wanted to show his friends. It was so important to him that he showed it to the first person he met at the school gate. Unfortunately, it was a Police Community Support Officer. This boy was permanently excluded, could not cope in the Pupil Referral Unit and at the end of Year 11 ended up with no qualifications. Most teachers would argue that this is not the typical behaviour of an adolescent who decided to take a knife into school. 'Innocent delinquency' is the term often used to describe this type of behaviour, which is characteristic of the FASD child.
(2) An 11-year-old girl upset her maths teacher by 'rudely' answering back in class in response to being told off for her behaviour and attitude. When the teacher attempted to quieten her by asking whether she thought the 'silly' comment she had made was funny, the 'rude' answer was, 'Yes, that's why I did it.' The child's reasoning was that the teacher had asked her a question and it would be rude not to answer and even ruder to lie! The silly comment that initiated the conversation has long been forgotten. However, the result was that she did not attend the classroom maths lessons for two terms. The FASD child frequently fails to understand adult sarcasm and often misinterprets every-day social communication.
(3) In nursery school, a three-year-old would scream and run away from the teaching assist-ant every time he saw her. This was after experiencing a whole day at nursery based on *The Gruffalo* children's story when the teaching assistant had dressed up as the Gruffalo. As a few of the younger children had been frightened, in order to reassure them the teaching assistant removed the costume's head. Most of the children were reassured except for this boy who was convinced that the teaching assistant *was* the Gruffalo. Distinguishing fantasy from reality can be a continuing struggle for the FASD child.

In April 2013, Raja Mukherjee and colleagues published an article outlining the impact that parenting a child with FASD has on their parents, carers and family life. The article did not focus solely on education, but its findings have significant implications for learning. The authors reported that affected children are different to parent in that traditional tried and tested parenting strategies have no or limited impact. The same conclusions can be directly applied to educational settings. Specifically, many affected pupils are difficult to teach and they learn differently. Conventional approaches to learning and teaching can often fail and very often have limited success.

If teachers are not aware of the best learning strategies to use and the reasons why the child's behaviour does not conform to expectations for the general student body, pupils affected by FASD can be incorrectly labelled as disruptive, defiant, lazy and, in the case of one of my daughters, then aged five, 'evil' – a case of inaccurate labelling that can rapidly become a self-fulfilling prophecy.

If teachers continue to apply the same sanctions week after week without modifying behaviour, then something has gone seriously wrong. In Scotland, during group discussion at an FASD awareness training event in Glasgow (2014), an adopter described the fortnightly cycle associated with her daughter's education. At the start of the first week the child did something that 'required' a short break-time detention. However, the student failed to attend and the detention was extended to lunchtime. Once again the child failed to attend because no one reminded her. Poor memory and organisational skills are characteristic of FASD. As time went by, the sanctions grew until by the end of the second week the child had a two to three fixed-term detention. The cycle then started again and the student learned nothing. Furthermore, she believed that once the detention had been served, everything would return to how it had been. In the teacher's mind this was not the case and she became more and more frustrated by repeated 'misbehaviour'. This is a classic example of the system trying harder, not differently, to the exasperation of all concerned.

Frustratingly, on being challenged, students will often be able to talk about why what they did was wrong and will give heartfelt assurances that they will not do it again. However, a common trait of FASD is impulsivity. Take, for example, the primary age pupil who was removed from on top of the lockers in a school corridor. The child was taken to the head teacher's office where the risks were explained. The head was reassured that it would never happen again. Twenty minutes later, the same pupil was on top of the same lockers. Sadly, the head and other staff were therefore convinced that the child was personally disobeying the school rules in order to undermine the staff. This caused huge tensions within the school, yet these convictions could not be further from the truth.

It is likely that the organically damaged brain was behaving impulsively. The child did not process the actions that led him to climb onto the lockers and therefore no reasoning was involved in what he did. When questioned, he knew that he needed to supply an answer but was only able to repeat the learned statements that he knew would please the staff. This pupil had not taken the decision to personally upset the head; as there was no cognitive processing, he could not remember why he had done it and was unable to explain himself. Hence, frustrations arose in the mind of the professionals who were attempting to rationalise the behaviours in terms of a typical undamaged brain, and this just does not work.

My own daughter lacks the emotional filters that most of us use to soften what we say or stop us from saying it at all. Without these filters, her comments can have very different reactions in the minds of those who hear them. Some teachers think that she is abrupt and rude. In Year 3 she told her teacher that the haircut she had had over the weekend made her look pretty. This engendered very positive feelings from the teacher. Two weeks later my daughter said that the dress the teacher was wearing that day made her look fat. This produced a totally different reaction, though it did not damage their relationship because the teacher understood the impulsivity. My daughter simply thought that she was being helpful in pointing out some facts to her teacher.

The inability of those affected by FASD to conform to the social norms associated with schools and school rules, unless they have repeated the behaviours and got them wrong numerous times, is frustrating but represents a direct indicator of how the damaged brain is functioning. To the affected child living in the 'black-and-white' world, their behaviours and reactions make logical sense. Often these have been considered and analysed within their framework of comprehension. The affected young person has little ability to modify what she or he does unless consistently supported by an understanding adult who acts as their 'external brain' for long periods of time.

It does not have to be this way but change requires teachers, lecturers and the whole educational establishment to accommodate the very specific learning needs of alcohol affected individuals. Where this is done successfully, individual students can and do reach their full potential. Where schools are unfamiliar with the best approaches, the story is far from positive, damaging the life chances of students and their families and in some cases costing society huge sums of money.

In their book on parenting children affected by FASD, Brown and Mather (2014) note that education dominates a significant portion of a child's and therefore a parent's life. Not all such children have significant learning difficulties. However, many parents still feel that they are 'falling through the cracks'; educationally their child is apparently able but emotionally and socially cannot fit in with her or his peers. Many parents feel that they are in a 'constant battle' around educational issues for their child. Living with these emotions and failures is unhealthy for the child and for everyone else concerned.

I invite readers to consider the neurological essence of learning, teaching and indeed parenting. If we distil teaching to the most basic and essential level, then what happens in the classroom is that we develop new neural pathways within the brain of the student (teaching) and strengthen them by repeating experiences (learning). But if we consider what is happening with children affected by FASD, we are attempting to secure new, strengthened, consistent neural pathways in an organically damaged brain. This means that teaching and learning strategies need to be amended to allow affected children to maximise their potential. Traditional learning strategies will often fail as the student's brain does not function like that of their peers.

What is needed to support affected children

This article has been written to signpost what has been successful in supporting affected pupils in schools throughout the education system. It is based on the last 10 years of supporting my girls and hundreds of other affected children and young people as well as their parents, carers and teachers across the UK.

It can only be an introduction as every school and college will need to develop their own learning plans to meet their requirements as well as the needs of individual affected students. More significantly, although there are general similarities in the way that FASD affects children in school, every case is different. As Phillips (2015) reports earlier in this journal, the impact of alcohol on the developing brain depends upon the amount consumed, the stage of pregnancy when it was consumed and the part of the brain which was developing at the time the mother was drinking. All affected pupils and students will fit somewhere on the 'spectrum', but FASD is not a constant and things will change over time. A key for success is building a sound relationship with individual students, taking time to listen to them and attempting to understand their perception of the world.

Some time ago, the US Department of Health and Human Services (2007) published *Reach to Teach: Educating elementary and middle school children with FASD*. The title of this guide, prepared for the Substance Abuse and Mental Health Services Administration (SAMHSA), clearly explains the route to success when working with affected children and young people. Professionals, be they teachers, teaching assistants or the parent, need to link with the child. Students with FASD cannot close the understanding gap themselves.

This sentiment is echoed in the UK in the work of Blackburn and colleagues (2012), who state in their book on educating children with FASD that 'sustainable learning can only occur when there is meaningful engagement' (Chapter 5). They go on to say that 'the process of engagement is a journey which connects the affected child to their environment (people, ideas, materials and concepts) so that learning can occur. If there is no connection then learning will not happen.' With affected children, it is the adult/teacher who needs to provide the bridge in order that these learning connections can be made. The unaffected people in a child's life provide the external brain to allow her or him to access learning.

It is not surprising that many proposals in the FASD Trust's guide for teachers of affected children (McGreavy, 2010) and the much more detailed guide for educating affected students published two years later (Blackburn, Carpenter and Egerton, 2014) are very similar. There is no 'one-size-fits-all' solution – indeed, something that works today may not work tomorrow – but despite these difficulties, teachers should be encouraged to develop and share with pupils and parents learning plans that develop some of these strategies.

The following is a list of strategies that have proved effective in supporting learners affected by FASD in school:

- Build a sound relationship with the individual student, taking time to listen to them and trying to understand them. The professionals need to work at making the connection with the young person as the student is unlikely to be able to bridge the gap constantly themselves.
- The school should provide a collegial environment where those working most closely with affected individuals can feel valued and supported.
- The greatest benefits come when all organisations and staff work together to support affected children and families.
- Often parents or carers of affected children know the child and how they react best. They are a key educational resource that schools need to cultivate, not blame.
- It is important to ensure that education professionals become the experts to support students, parents and carers.
- Effective, real-time, honest and open communication between school and home is essential.
- Modify educational expectations of what the affected children will be able to do. Many will not be able to operate within the normally expected behaviours of their non-affected peers.
- If one way of teaching is not working then change the way that you expect the child to learn.
- Try not to analyse the behaviour of affected students in terms of what is typical and logical social behaviour. What they say is often not what they actually mean or what they can do.
- Best results will occur where there is a strong, understanding relationship between the pupil and trusted adults, who can act as the pupil's external brain to help them pause and make the right decisions.
- Manage any change carefully and sensitively, including the pupil in planning change at the earliest instance.

- Develop a nurturing learning environment where visual distractions are kept to a minimum.
- Provide opportunities for small group work in a supportive environment.
- Keep instructions short and simple and build on what the child can already do.
- Pre-tutor the child so that they have some idea of what is going to happen.
- Use a range of visual and kinaesthetic learning opportunities; demonstrate rather than tell children what to do.
- Encourage success by recognising positive behaviour immediately with praise and a concrete reward. Sanctions that rely on delayed actions will often prove to be ineffective.
- Use positive, direct, consistent language in instructions and use the child's name.
- Give the child time to think about the instructions you have given.
- Break up activities with physical movement.
- Try to personalise questions by including the child's name or familiar information or objects.
- Use templates that structure the work you expect from the child.
- Provide clear and consistently applied rules throughout the school.
- Ensure that all adults are aware of the strategies that are being applied to support the pupil.
- Decide whether breaking school/class rules is deliberate, due to a lack of understanding or to the child becoming distracted or to whether they cannot remember what is expected of them.

The title of this article comes from a fridge magnet that my youngest affected daughter gave to her Year 6 class teacher when she left her very supportive and nurturing primary school: 'I know that I'm in my own world; it's OK, they know me here.' These 15 words perfectly sum up everything to do with her life. Her condition cannot be cured, but by attempting to enter her world for a period, strategies can be developed that will promote sound learning most of the time. My daughter's world is not an easy place to reach and is still harder to understand. Often she just cannot comprehend the learning environments that her school has created and needs an adult to act as her 'external brain' to guide her; she needs adults who can reach into her world and mould her learning so that she is able to access ours.

The absence of research in the UK

Many articles that deal with conditions that affect children's ability to learn are grounded in a large and developing body of academic research and peer-reviewed practical experience. Regrettably, this is not the case with the impact that FASD can have on individual pupils, their peers, teachers or schools, at least in the UK. There is almost no research at all and much of the published material relates to work undertaken in the USA or Canada where education systems are very different.

Luciana Berger MP, speaking during the Foetal Alcohol Syndrome debate in Westminster Hall in October 2014, observed that in the UK 'there is no systematic record of the needs of children with FASD and no official guidance on best educational strategies' (Berger, 2014). Later in the debate a number of MPs contrasted this with the situation in Canada. In addition, the support offered by the education system varies across the UK where practice has developed in an ad hoc way. Consequently, we can only draw limited conclusions as to how far adapting teaching and the school environment has been successful in meeting the learning needs of affected students.

The experience of working in the UK

Much of what is discussed here seeks to contextualise the research from overseas with examples drawn from practical experiences of working with and supporting many affected children, their families and schools throughout England, Wales and Scotland.

The most important message is that it cannot be the role of any one individual or organisation to provide the necessary support. The greatest benefits come when all organisations and staff work together, with schools as one part of this partnership. In England the new Education, Health and Care plans have the potential to offer a stronger more integrated approach to supporting affected children until they are 25.

Working with parents and carers

Parents often have the greatest knowledge of and emotional connection with the young people affected. Schools, social workers and clinicians who ignore experienced parents or carers are quite likely to fail the student. Mukherjee and colleagues (2013) showed that every parent and carer who contributed to their research had been blamed for the behaviour of their child on one or more occasion. It is common for parents to report that schools have suggested they would benefit from parenting classes – misguided advice because parenting classes based on traditional behaviour management (praising good and ignoring bad) do not work for the FASD child.

One of the main frustrations endured by parents stems from having to explain time and time again what FASD is and how it affects their child. In seeking help, they have become experts on the disorder even though they do not relish this role. One major improvement would be to increase professionals' awareness of the condition. Indeed, as a family, the biggest weight taken from our shoulders was when we changed primary schools and my daughters were enrolled in one where the head teacher and our GP were the adopters of affected children; we no longer needed to explain ourselves or to educate.

Not every parent will be this fortunate, and effective, honest and open communication between school and home is essential. Secure learning will only happen where there is consistency in the approaches taken in both settings. This needs to be developed and sustained throughout the time that the affected child is in education.

In the US state of Maryland, the national FASD Center for Excellence has produced proforma sheets to facilitate two-way conversations between home and school on a daily basis (Department of Health and Human Services, 2007). In the UK, effective systems use school exercise books as a two-way diary. Equally successful has been the one-to-one, face-to-face contact that happens at the 'classroom door' in most UK primary schools. In secondary schools, email communication is effective, provided it is channelled through a single point of contact. Sometimes this is the form tutor, but more often it is a key teaching assistant who has been formally identified and trained.

The impact on the teacher

After parents and carers, teachers and classroom assistants are often most affected by the impact of a child with FASD. They are in contact with the affected child on a daily basis, juggling his or her learning needs with those of other pupils. This is a difficult task and to minimise resulting stress, staff need opportunities to share their experiences and receive support. Mukherjee and colleagues (2013) reported that parenting affected children can be isolating, an experience that can equally affect teachers.

Reframing expectations

All schools and colleges have expectations about how pupils and students will behave and the majority will fulfil these with no more than a minor hiccup along the way. But for many affected children, school life is not this smooth and often they will repeat errors and behaviours that teachers have attempted to explain, modify and correct on numerous occasions. This can lead to huge frustrations for everyone involved.

Mary Mather (2012) uses the following diagram to illustrate how reframing expectations of how the affected child might respond in school can improve their overall achievement.

If everyone involved with the child or young person could think about them in terms of the expectations expressed on the right-hand side of Figure 1 rather than the left, then the ways in which affected children are managed and approached in their learning and how behaviours are modified would be quite different.

The impact on the child

There is stigma associated with an FASD diagnosis. Eventually all affected children will need to have their disability explained to them in an age-appropriate way and schools will have to support the child in this process.

Children are repeatedly told by parents, friends, relatives and teachers that school is important. Those who have been in care will have heard it from designated teachers, social workers, reviewing officers, foster carers and even health care staff. No child sets out to fail in school. They try hard to succeed but struggle with the fact that they react

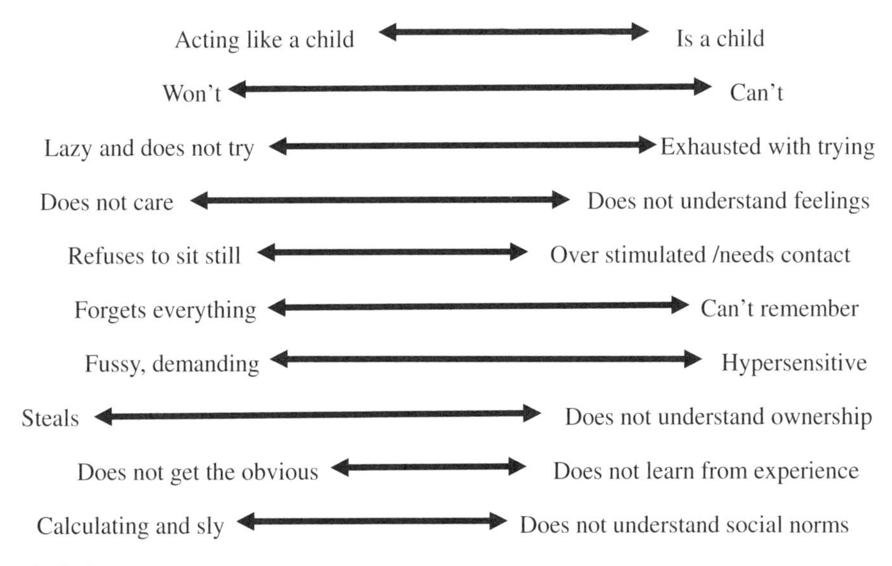

Figure 1. Reframing expectations.

and learn differently. They know that they cannot behave like their unaffected friends and cannot make the changes that are expected of them.

Bedford Borough Council's Youth Service (2010) carried out work with affected teenagers as part of an FASD project. The key points to emerge were: they feared growing up; were confused and frustrated; understood the challenges they faced; were worried about the future; and knew that they could not cope and were not in control. If this is added to the general angst of being a teenager, it is easy to understand why children with FASD struggle and become frustrated.

Although not all affected children have special educational needs, the gap between their educational achievement and that of their peers becomes more apparent with age. In England, pupils who coped in the primary years suddenly cannot cope with the complex demands of secondary education. Teachers often question why the student did not have an educational statement at primary school because they can no longer access learning. This sudden change in ability to cope means that schools struggle to support children.

Children with FASD find any change difficult. They like consistency as it supports those neural pathways which have been constructed in their damaged brains. Change is disruptive and destabilising. The transition points between school phases as well as from one year to another require sensitive handling. An affected child cannot be expected to behave like her or his peers.

At the time of writing, it is six weeks into the new term and my daughter has not managed to attend all five lessons in any given school day. Even though her school has been at pains to keep the changes she will experience to the absolute minimum, she cannot cope with some of the new subject teachers and the changes of students in class.

Even more worryingly, the following quotation from an email from an adoptive mother and experienced parent shows how bad things can get: 'Her behaviour is escalating and she is increasingly harming us and now herself. She is off school again today and I have no idea when we will get her back' (personal communication, September 2014). This is by no means an isolated case and the problems associated with school can just be the tip of a very big iceberg.

Home education

A significant number of affected children and young people are currently being taken out of school and home educated. This a valid course of action if it meets the educational needs of the child and the skills set of the family. However, more and more parents are making this decision because they believe that the education system, be it mainstream or special schools, cannot cope with or meet the needs of their children. Home education is seen as a last resort when the parents feel that the experiences they are having in school are damaging their child.

This is not the best reason for making such a decision and clearly reflects a breakdown in communication between the education system and parents. Home education offers little opportunity for affected children to learn to socialise with their peers. It also prevents their peers from understanding that the disability caused by alcohol consumption during pregnancy is life-long. In almost every case, the affected child will outlive their parents; if society has not become aware of the condition and its impact, those affected will be left without the supports they need in middle age. Making society aware cannot be left to luck. It is important that FASD is covered by all students in the personal, social and health education curriculum. Indeed, the MPs made this point in the Westminster debate previously cited.

Conclusion

We are starting to see a slow change in the UK. Parts of the country are gradually waking up to the condition and increasing numbers of affected children are being identified. Although a diagnosis is desirable, it is a start and not the end. Parents and carers do not always wish to be the experts when it comes to dealing with children affected by FASD. It is hard enough providing safe, consistent and supportive parenting without having to educate those who are meant to be supporting these youngsters in school.

We need to develop a system in the UK where all the services needed to support families are in one place and working together to promote the best outcomes possible for affected children. Training and best practice should be shared with everyone. If we fail to do this, we will continue to waste money on tackling crisis situations as they arise when much less could be spent earlier on managing the condition. One affected 12-year-old in an English local authority was returned to care because his adoptive family could no longer cope, despite trying their hardest. This sad outcome is likely to lead to a massive waste of potential in a child who, if support had been established earlier, could have achieved much more, as well as being a drain on welfare budgets.

Affected children can be happy in their own educational world and can achieve but professionals, if they are to help them make the kind of progress that we and they desire, need to join them. Waiting for them to join us in the world with which we are familiar will be a long and ultimately frustrating experience.

Notes

1. The role of the virtual school head teacher is to support and improve the educational attainment of children and young people in care who are in mainstream schools. The idea was first introduced by the UK Labour Government in 2007. Today the post of virtual school head is statutory for all local authorities.
2. The pupil premium comprises additional funding for publicly funded schools in England to raise the attainment of disadvantaged pupils and close the gap between them and their peers.
3. This stems from personal knowledge as the author was a school governor at the primary school concerned.

References

All Party Parliamentary Group (2012) *Education Matters in Care: A report by the independent cross-party inquiry into the educational attainment of looked after children in England.* London: UK Parliament. Available at: http://dera.ioe.ac.uk/15782/.

Bedford Borough Council Youth Service (2010) *FASD Project.* Unpublished.

Berger L (2014) Foetal Alcohol Syndrome debate. Column 41WH. Available at: www.publications.parliament.uk/pa/cm201415/cmhansrd/cm141014/halltext/141014h0001.htm#141014h0001.htm_spnew40.

Blackburn C, Carpenter B and Egerton J (2012) *Educating Children and Young People with Foetal Alcohol Spectrum Disorders: Constructing personalised pathways to learning.* Abingdon: Routledge.

Brown J and Mather M (2014) *Foetal Alcohol Spectrum Disorder: Parenting a child with an invisible disability.* Oxford: FASD Trust.

Department for Education (2012) *Schools Funding Settlement including Pupil Premium: 2013 to 2014 financial year.* National Archives. Available at: http://webarchive.nationalarchives.gov.uk/20130123124929/http://www.education.gov.uk/schools/adminandfinance/financialmanagement/schoolsrevenuefunding/a00218077/funding-settlement-2013-14.

Department for Education (2014) *Pupil Premium 2014 to 2015: Conditions of grant*. Available at: www.gov.uk/government/uploads/system/uploads/attachment_data/file/283193/Pupil_Premium_CoG_2014-15.pdf.

Department of Health and Human Services (2007) *Reach to Teach: Educating elementary and middle school children with Fetal Alcohol Spectrum Disorders*. Rockville, MD: Substance Abuse and Mental Health Services Administration. Available at: http://fasdcenter.samhsa.gov/documents/reach_to_teach_final_011107.pdf.

McGreavy I (2010) *Foetal Alcohol Spectrum Disorders: A guide for teachers*. Oxford: FASD Trust.

Mather M (2012) *FASD – Implications for Practice*. The FASD Trust Medical & Healthcare Professionals' Forum. Local Open Study Day, Peterborough, 23 November. Unpublished.

Mukherjee R, Wray E, Commers M, Hollins S and Curfs L (2013) The impact of raising a child with FASD upon carers: findings from a mixed methodology study in the UK. *Adoption & Fostering* 37(1): 43–56.

Brian Roberts is an independent trainer and consultant specialising in supporting and improving the life chances of vulnerable children and young people. He has been a local authority foster carer for over 20 years and is a special guardian with a number of affected children living with him. He provides education advice to the FASD Trust and is Chair of the Fostering Networks England Advisory Committee.

Article

Adoption & Fostering
2015, Vol. 39(3) 247–255

DOI: 10.1177/0308575915599096
adoptionfostering.sagepub.com

The challenges of caring for a child with FASD

Julia Brown
The FASD Trust, UK

Abstract
'Caring for a child or young person with foetal alcohol spectrum disorders (FASD) is very challenging' is a statement commonly heard by the parents/carers involved. But why is it so challenging? What are the specific challenges? How does this sentence relate to the family-finding team, to panel considerations, to training for foster carers, to the selection of adopters and to care planning? This article seeks to address some of these issues from the viewpoint of the author's experience of parenting two children with FASD and also as the Chief Executive of the FASD Trust, a national charity supporting affected children and their families/carers in the UK.

Keywords
FASD, disability, challenges, support, outcomes

Diagnosing a child with FASD

The first and biggest challenge for this group of children and young people is the failure of many professionals and UK society to recognise their disability. As reflected in the title of this special edition, we deliberately called our book on parenting these children, *Parenting a Child with an **Invisible** Disability* (Brown and Mather, 2014). When a child is looked after, there is a tendency to focus upon her or his experiences since birth and a failure to recognise that they were born with a permanent, untreatable condition and subsequently suffered secondary neglect and abuse that have added to their problems.

These children often look 'normal'. Not all those affected by FASD have the diagnostic facial features associated with pre-natal alcohol exposure. Some have slight features that are not necessarily instantly discernible, especially to the untrained eye. However, absence of apparent physical differences and facial features does not mean an absence of disability. Although some affected children have learning difficulties, others are very verbal with good, expressive language. They may have a reading ability above their actual age and an IQ within the normal range.

Corresponding author:
Julia Brown, the FASD Trust, Unit 8, the Gallery, 54 Marston Street, Oxford OX4 1LF, UK.
Email: juliabrown@fasdtrust.co.uk

One agency carried out a study of the mental health needs of children on a concurrent planning programme (Coram, 2012). The children had been removed at birth and placed with carers who were approved to foster and then adopt them should the courts rule that they were unable to return to their birth families. These babies had suffered no trauma, abuse or neglect and remained in the same placement. Several of them were fractious, irritable infants, difficult to soothe and to establish feeding patterns for – all the 'classic' symptoms of a child exposed prenatally to alcohol or drugs.

One family we supported through our work at the FASD Trust was sympathetically told by school that they fully understood that their adopted child's behaviour was due to trauma and neglect in early life. The school were somewhat taken aback when they were informed that the child had lived with the adopters since being discharged from hospital at the age of three weeks and that the emotional and behavioural problems they were seeing were not the result of neglectful experiences but of a disability called FASD (Oldham Support Group, 2014).

Lack of information

The second issue that families face is a lack of documentation about exposure to alcohol. Social workers often fail to document alcohol misuse and to inform substitute carers of the risk that the child will be affected. FASD is a 'spectrum' with varying degrees of severity and the difficulties will not be apparent in a baby or toddler. Most children present with problems at around the age of six but others can be teenagers before the full extent of their difficulties becomes apparent.

This lack of documentation leads to the next challenge faced by many substitute carers: obtaining an accurate diagnosis for the child in their care. There is a tendency to document drug misuse and to be concerned about women taking drugs during pregnancy. Drugs are illegal and therefore deemed 'more dangerous' than alcohol, which being legal is regarded erroneously as 'safe'. From a medical perspective, neither drugs nor alcohol should be consumed during pregnancy but alcohol has the greater potential to cause harm to the developing foetus. Drugs and alcohol go together like fish and chips; an individual's journey into drug misuse will invariably involve alcohol as well. There are no UK figures on how many children on child protection registers or placed for adoption, or in other permanent placements outside the birth family, have a family history involving the excessive consumption of alcohol.

Lack of support

Another consequence of failing to recognise alcohol misuse in the mother is that she will not be offered any help and may well go on to have further children. If she continues to drink, each subsequent child will be more affected than the previous one; her first born will be the least affected and her youngest the most affected by FASD, with each successive child in between being sequentially further along the severity scale of the spectrum. The needs of each new child will therefore increase and with it the demands upon the substitute carer. Furthermore, in the absence of diagnosis there is a tendency to place siblings together. In the FASD Trust we are aware of three, four and even five siblings placed in the same adoptive family.

The medical research literature is quite clear: there is a direct correlation between maternal age and level of disability (Durkin, et al., 2008; Grether, et al., 2009; Saha, et al., 2009; Tsuchiya, et al., 2008). The older the mother, the more likely it is that the child will be affected by FASD. We also know that FASD is dose related – the more alcohol a child is exposed to in utero the more likely they are to be affected and the more severe their disability. In addition, as time passes, the mother needs to consume greater quantities of alcohol in order to achieve the same 'fix'.

The burden on carers

It is important that family-finders do not overburden permanent substitute carers, who are already under enormous pressure. This will only lead to placement disruption or carers literally hanging in there by the skin of their teeth. The capacity of carers' ability to fully appreciate and truly cope with the reality of the demands of a sibling group with FASD must be thoroughly explored before placement and before they are offered another sibling. Potential adopters and long-term foster carers must have a clear understanding of FASD, its impact on the child's development and the reality of life with these endearing but very demanding children.

The 'blame game'

Another of the common misconceptions we encounter through our work at the FASD Trust, and a major challenge faced by many affected by FASD, is the 'blame game' of the undiagnosed child. This takes many forms. The placement is thought to be at fault and so the child is moved. The social worker is thought to be at fault and another one assigned to the case. The school is thought to be wrong for the child and the school is changed. In the worst-case scenario, the children themselves are 'blamed' and labelled as 'oppositional defiant' and eventually 'unable to be placed in a family'.

The perils of misdiagnosis

Social work practice over the last 15 to 20 years has been dominated by attachment theory. In our experience in the FASD Trust, the inappropriate use of this theory has led to many carers feeling isolated, guilty and incorrectly labelled as over-anxious, inadequate parents. The children then become increasingly confused and unhappy as inappropriate interventions and therapies are offered for an unrecognised disability. The reality is that these children are not disobedient and defiant but *disabled*. Whoever they are and wherever they live, whoever cares for them, whoever is their social worker or teacher, the child will display these behaviours as symptoms of their disability.

Recognising and diagnosing FASD early will save the local authority, and the taxpayer in general, considerable sums of money and enables the funding available to be spent more effectively – an increasingly salient issue in these times of budget constraints. More importantly, it opens the way for these children and young people to achieve emotionally, behaviourally and academically their potential, leading to placements that are not disrupted but stable.

The work of Professor Ann Streissguth from the University of Washington, who carried out research on a large cohort over a period of many years, clearly demonstrates the link between age of diagnosis and appropriate support in relation to outcomes for the FASD affected individual as an adult, showing a direct correlation between early diagnosis and better adult outcomes (Streissguth, et al., 1997).

Historically, those caring for children with FASD have endured tortuous diagnostic journeys and multiple, usually ineffective interventions. At long last, more of the medical community in the UK are recognising and understanding the condition. However, the challenge of ensuring an appropriate support package for the child and their carers after diagnosis remains.

Accessing the right support

So, once we have recognised and diagnosed FASD, what support do those affected and their carers need? How can we spend our increasingly limited financial resources wisely and ensure the best outcomes? What are the day-to-day challenges faced by those caring for children with FASD? How do we ensure that placements do not break down?

The first common hurdle is the belief that this is a condition that can be fixed, something the child will grow out of, or that all will be well once a loving, stable home has been found. But FASD is a lifelong but not a life-shortening disability. There is no cure or fix. It is a condition that needs to be managed, or as the Canadians put it, the children and their families need 'strategies not solutions' (Alberta Children's Services, Jones and Cunningham, 2004).

Children and young people affected by FASD desperately require stability and permanence, as many of the strategies to help them and the lifelong support networks they will need take time to establish. The support will need to be readjusted as the child grows and their requirements change. Multiple placement moves must be avoided at all costs and permanency, in whatever legal framework is appropriate, sought as swiftly as possible.

One of the biggest hindrances to these children and young people receiving appropriate support is the faulty expectations of the adults around them. A key finding from much of the US research has been that having a primary caregiver who understands FASD and advocates appropriately for the right interventions constitutes a major factor towards positive outcomes in adulthood (O'Connor, et al., 2006; Riley, et al., 2011).

Adopters dreaming of the type of normal family life experienced by their friends need to be fully prepared, so that they truly understand the challenges of parenting a child with FASD. All foster carers need relevant training as a significant percentage of the children they will care for, both now and in the future, are likely to be affected. Social workers and panel members must appreciate the complexity and lifelong nature of FASD to enable them to make informed decisions and offer appropriate long-term support to these children and their substitute carers. Very few local authorities currently offer adequate training to these groups, tending to play down the multifaceted nature of the condition.

When assessing prospective adopters or other long-term substitute carers for children with FASD, consideration must be given to the strength and diversity of their wider support networks. The key question is, 'How will they support you in parenting a child with a permanent disability?' There is a significant difference between a child who has been traumatised or abused, and for whom love, stability and appropriate professional therapy will make significant changes so that she or he can move forwards, hopefully to experience an independent and successful adult life, and the child affected by FASD. These children have a permanent disability which is not 'curable', and will require support and 'parenting' for many years, or even their whole lifetime. We have met grandparents unwilling even to babysit the FASD child because they are so challenging, but who are more than happy to care for their other typically developing grandchildren.

One of the major practical issues faced by the carers of children with FASD is having sufficient physical energy to manage the daily practical requirements of looking after them. Younger children especially are often diagnosed with ADHD. Their activity and energy levels are high; they seem to crave movement and struggle to sit still and focus on a task, unless it is a favourite TV programme or activity in which they become wholly absorbed. Many have sleeping difficulties, exacerbated by their previous inconsistent, chaotic lifestyles and early trauma. They can have frequent nightmares. In the early years, their immune system is poor, leaving a perpetual round of illness and time off school and work to manage.

Caring for those affected by FASD is physically and emotionally demanding. Walking, talking, toilet training, all the major early milestones are often achieved late or towards the upper end of normal. In school-aged children, their ability to speak well usually masks their incapacity to understand what is said to them, and their ability to read fluently disguises their inability to comprehend what they have read. Their receptive language, their ability to understand what is being said to them, is delayed and often half their chronological age.

Pre-natal alcohol exposure affects the fine motor more than the gross motor skills, which means that children can struggle to dress themselves in the early years; buttons and zips are difficult to manage. They have problems holding a pencil and writing. They struggle with spatial awareness, which, combined with balance issues, often leads to them being labelled as clumsy and accident prone. When younger children have poor muscle tone and skeletal deformities, an assessment by a physiotherapist is recommended. Exercises and activities such as swimming or horse-riding can help. As muscle tone improves, the child will find it easier to sit still and some of their restless 'ADHD tendencies' will recede.

These children present challenging behaviours and they do not learn from their mistakes. So-called traditional parenting techniques have no impact or merely serve to make the situation worse. The children suffer from sensory processing and integration disorders culminating in sensory overload that manifests as tantrums or emotional eruptions. They either do not realise they are hungry, so do not eat, or do not stop eating. Occupational therapy may be of value here, recommending effective interventions for implementation in a variety of settings, including school.

There are increased possibilities that children will meet the diagnostic criteria for autism, ADHD, dyspraxia, conduct disorder or attachment disorders. The list is endless and the multiple potential diagnoses add to parents' increasing distress. As we have seen, FASD is often said to be an invisible disability, not only because the child appears physically normal but also because some of their difficulties can be subtle or not evident, hidden by the perception that they have ability, whereas the reality is they have no *capability*.

Seeking appropriate interventions

This is where people caring for children affected by FASD face two other challenges: first, to ensure that others, particularly professionals, fully appreciate their child's actual difficulties; and second, to make sure that the interventions offered are appropriate.

For example, the affected children are often extremely talkative, leading to the false assumption that this is a child who is intelligent and who does not have any speech and language problems. When properly analysed it becomes apparent that their speech is often repetitive or echolalic. A speech and language assessment can actually be useful to gauge the child's receptive language level. Speech and language therapists can also advise and assist with social and conversation competence, taking turns and making friends – skills that all children with FASD struggle to learn.

Another common intervention for the undiagnosed child, especially if she or he is or previously has been looked after and has had traumatic experiences in early life, is to offer 'talking therapies' to enable them to overcome their difficulties. However, the child with FASD often struggles to properly engage with the therapy; they do not understand the abstract concepts being discussed. In addition, they are being 'talked to' in language that is above their receptive language level; they fail to comprehend, fail to engage and fail to change. Children with FASD do not have a concept of time and so often struggle to put events into context and in a clear timeframe. Their short-term memory can be especially poor while their longer-term memory has a tendency to operate on a 'random recall' basis. A child may have heard someone use a phrase or sentence in a particular context, only to repeat it in the wrong circumstances. This also impacts on their ability to engage with talking therapy aimed at helping them come to terms with past events.

When therapy is unsuccessful, the family is likely to move on into the whole blame cycle: Is it the therapy, the therapist, the carers or the social worker's fault? The fact that the child was born with untreatable brain damage and cannot process information is rarely considered as an option.

Children and young people with FASD need a multi-disciplinary support package from professionals who understand these disorders. This package needs to be reviewed regularly and adjusted over time to meet the needs of the child as she or he grows. The kind of support that is appropriate and required by a five-year-old is not necessarily the same as that suitable for a child at 11 years old. But it is also important not to overburden carers and those with FASD with multiple appointments and professionals, all giving conflicting advice. Ideally, one professional should take the lead on behalf of the child or young person and their carers.

These complex, demanding, challenging, lovable children eventually leave their primary caregivers physically and emotionally exhausted. While I understand and wholly support the requirement to look within a birth family for alternative carers when birth parents are unable to provide care, I seriously question the wisdom of placing young, very demanding children with elderly grandparents whose ability to cope will be compromised by their increasing age.

Support for life

There are also longer-term considerations to be addressed. Children affected by FASD require some degree of support for life. About one-third always will need 24-hour help or high levels of care; another third will require supported independence and a third will manage independence with occasional assistance. As a general rule, the children with FASD coming into the care system tend to be in the first two categories, mainly because they have usually been exposed to higher levels of alcohol. Alcohol damage is then combined with other in-utero stresses such as drugs, tobacco and domestic violence in pregnancy. Finally, post-birth trauma, placement moves, neglect and abuse mean that their disability is likely to be at the severe end of the spectrum. A significant number of looked after children with FASD will never be able to leave care and live independently.

Substitute carers need the resources to continue caring, even when the 'child' is in their 20s and 30s, yet there are virtually no services for vulnerable adults with FASD. This is not a life-limiting condition; it is permanent with a normal life expectancy. Having removed these children from birth families where, traditionally, long-term support would be provided by the family unit, surely it is incumbent upon the 'corporate parents' to ensure that enduring services and support are available? As so often, financial pressures tend to influence decisions that need to be taken.

Carers need respite, but most local authorities only offer it to the parents of children with severe physical difficulties. Others have a misconception that what needs to be provided is an expensive, monthly weekend package of care. The reality is that carers usually only need a few hours a week or a babysitter to enable parents to go out for an evening. These children do not cope well with change. They are inflexible in their thinking and can respond to new developments with emotional outbursts and tantrums. Parents therefore usually want someone to stay with the child in their own home. They also need consistency of respite carer. Most importantly, this temporary carer needs to understand FASD and the high level of supervision that such children require. They must be someone in whom the primary caregivers have confidence. Very few respite care services provide this type of reliable, flexible and individually tailored care, yet it could prevent a placement breakdown or adoption disruption.

Caring for the older child

Another challenge faced by those caring for teenagers, particularly in foster care, is the expectation that reaching the age of 14 or 15 will automatically lead to them being given more independence and freedom. As a general rule, these young people operate emotionally and socially at around half their chronological age. They have a poor sense of danger, poor impulse control, are easily led and naïve, and inadequate supervision or too much freedom is a recipe for disaster. Carers often find themselves described as over anxious and over protective in conflict with the teenager's social worker. The reality is that the carers' instincts and concerns should be taken seriously. We have known young people who have been overlooked or dismissed to go missing, to become involved with the police, to be raped and even, in one tragic case, killed.

The vulnerability of this group should never be underestimated and steps need to be taken to help young people with FASD to move towards 'supported interdependence'. This presents huge challenges for agencies as they struggle with the complexity of enabling them to have a social life, learn life skills and live with some independence, and keeping them physically and emotionally safe.

Outcomes

Based on long-term US research and looking at the experiential evidence we have gained from the increasing number of young people with FASD now reaching adulthood in the UK, the most positive outcomes are achieved by two groups: children who were diagnosed when they were very young and who have stayed in the same supportive placement; and children who 'know and own' their condition (Blackburn and Whitehurst, 2010; Loock, et al., 2005; Mukherjee, et al., 2013; Streissguth, et al., 1996).

In the same way in which it is widely acknowledged that it is better to tell a child early that they are adopted, so it is easier if a child learns when they are younger that they have FASD. They need to know what the condition is and how it affects them. In this way, they become accustomed to understanding why they struggle with some issues and whom to ask for help.

It eliminates a lot of confusion, frustration and fear when young adults understand why they are 'different' from their peers. This, in turn, impacts positively on their behaviour, self-esteem and anxiety levels.

Individuals with FASD will always have to ask someone else to help or assist them with various aspects of life. For instance, many will be unable to manage money, pay bills, take out contracts for mobile phones or have bank accounts. Like time or distance, money is an abstract concept that young people with FASD struggle to understand. Children who do not know what is wrong with them do very badly as they move into adult life. Knowledge is also a safeguarding issue, as it allows children time to learn and recognise who are the 'safe' or appropriate people to ask for assistance.

There used to be a perception that those with FASD were disobedient, disruptive children whom no one would foster or adopt and who in all likelihood would grow up to be alcoholic, drug-addicted criminals, ending their lives homeless, jobless and perhaps committing suicide. However, children with FASD have many positive qualities. They are often creative, both musically and artistically. They are endearing, affectionate, loving children who enjoy being involved in activities and family life. They just struggle to know how to get involved in a socially appropriate manner. They have a great deal to offer the world. A significant number of parents and carers successfully enjoy parenting those with FASD. The most successful placements are where parents have adopted or fostered with a full understanding of the condition and how it is likely to affect the child coming into their care.

FASD is a complex disability that we are only just beginning to grapple with in the UK, especially within social care. We are also starting to recognise that it disproportionately affects looked after children. In fact, it is probably a major yet largely unrecognised contributing factor to some of the poor outcomes we consistently see for young people leaving the care system in comparison to their peers.

While improvements have undoubtedly been made, it must be noted that the UK still significantly lags behind its global partners such as the USA, Canada, Australia, South Africa, both in terms of giving clear advice to pregnant women about alcohol consumption in pregnancy and recognising and diagnosing FASD.

As we finally identify and diagnose FASD more accurately, it is imperative that we seriously look at how we can support those affected to ensure far better outcomes. With its comprehensive universal social care systems, the UK has the potential to become a world leader in this area. That process will begin by all of us, both at a personal and an organisational/statutory level, ensuring that we fully understand this condition and its impact on individuals with the condition. We must also take time to reflect on our own professional practice, ensuring that we are doing our best to adapt and improve our work and the services offered to those affected.

Ultimately, these children and young people were born into a society that could not prevent them from being born with a disability but that can, at least, offer them every chance of reaching their potential and having success in life.

References

Alberta Children's Services, Jones S and Cunningham L (2004) *FASD: Strategies, Not Solutions.* Available at: www.faslink.org/strategies_not_solutions.pdf.

Blackburn C and Whitehurst T (2010) Foetal alcohol spectrum disorders (FASD): raising awareness in early years settings. *British Journal of Special Education* 37(3): 122–129.

Brown J and Mather M (2014) *Foetal Alcohol Spectrum Disorder: Parenting a child with an invisible disability*. Oxford: FASD Trust.
Coram (2012) *Concurrent Planning Study: Interim report*. London: Coram. Available at: www.coram.org.uk/sites/default/files/resource_files/Concurrent%20Planning%20Study%202012.pdf.
Durkin MS, Maenner CJ, Newschaffer CJ, et al. (2008) Advanced parental age and the risk of autism spectrum disorder. *American Journal of Epidemiology* 168(11): 1268–1276.
Grether JK, Anderson MC, Croen AL, et al. (2009) Risk of autism and increasing maternal and paternal age in a large North American population. *American Journal of Epidemiology* 170(9): 1118–1126.
Loock C, Conry J, Cook JL, et al. (2005) Identifying fetal alcohol spectrum disorder in primary care. *Canadian Medical Association Journal* 172(5): 628–630.
Mukherjee R, Wray E, Commers M, et al. (2013) The impact of raising a child with FASD upon carers: findings from a mixed methodology study in the UK. *Adoption & Fostering* 37(1): 43–56.
O'Connor MJ, Frankel F, Paley B, et al. (2006) A controlled social skills training for children with fetal alcohol spectrum disorders. *Journal of Consulting and Clinical Psychology* 74(4): 639–648.
Oldham Support Group (2014) FASD Trust. Confidential information.
Riley EP, Clarren S, Weinberg J and Jonsson E (eds) (2011) *Fetal Alcohol Spectrum Disorder: Management and policy perspectives of FASD*. Weinheim: Wiley/VCH Verlag & Co.
Saha S, Barnett AG, Foldi C, et al. (2009) Advanced paternal age is associated with impaired neuro-cognitive outcomes during infancy and childhood. *PLOS Medicine*. doi: 10.1371/journal.pmed.1000040.
Streissguth AP, Barr HM, Kogan J and Bookstein FL (1996) *Understanding the Occurrence of Secondary Disabilities in Clients with Fetal Alcohol Syndrome (FAS) and Fetal Alcohol Effects (FAE): Final report to the Centers for Disease Control and Prevention (CDC)*. Seattle: University of Washington, Fetal Alcohol & Drug Unit, Tech. Rep. No. 96-06.
Streissguth AP, Barr H, Kogan J and Bookstein F (eds) (1997) Primary and secondary disabilities in fetal alcohol syndrome. In: Streissguth AP and Kanter J (eds) *The Challenge of Fetal Alcohol Syndrome: Overcoming secondary disability*. Washington, DC: University of Washington Press, pp. 25–39.
Tsuchiya KJ, Matsumoto K, Miyachi T, et al. (2008) Paternal age at birth and high-functioning autistic-spectrum disorder in offspring. *The British Journal of Psychiatry* 193(4): 316–321.

Julia Brown is an adoptive mother of three children and co-founder with her husband of the FASD Trust, based in Oxford (www.fasdtrust.co.uk). She writes and lectures widely on FASD, in particular its impact on family life and professional practice. Further useful contacts in the UK are the All Party Parliamentary Group for FASD (www.appg-fasd.org.uk) and for professionals seeking help, the forthcoming Oxford Foundation for FASD (www.oxfordfoundation-FASD.com).

Article

Adoption & Fostering
2015, Vol. 39(3) 256–262

DOI: 10.1177/0308575915599862
adoptionfostering.sagepub.com

Progress in addressing FASD in Scotland[1]

Margaret Watts
NHS Western Isles, Scotland, UK

Abstract

In Scotland, despite high levels of alcohol use by women, public awareness and professional knowledge of the risks of drinking while pregnant are low and there has been very little research into foetal alcohol spectrum disorders (FASD) and their effects. Recently, however, the Scottish Government has shown leadership with the commissioning of an FASD e-learning resource from NHS Education Scotland, the development of a toolkit for FASD Awareness Day and the planned institution of two two-day intensive training courses for health and social care professionals in the recognition, assessment, diagnosis and support of children affected by foetal alcohol harm. This article charts some of these developments.

Keywords

FASD, Scotland, training

Introduction

Worldwide it is estimated that FASD affects around one in every 100 births (May and Gossage, 2001). In Scotland, in part because the conditions forming the spectrum are poorly recognised, despite high levels of alcohol use in women and therefore a high potential for harm to occur, the incidence is unknown. Awareness of the condition among the general public across the UK is poor (Mukherjee, et al., 2015). Furthermore, professional knowledge and awareness are low (Carswell, 2007; Mukherjee, et al., 2013) with health and social care professionals having experienced working with a child with FASD on only a few occasions, not feeling comfortable in making the diagnosis and in understanding effective management. However, there is an appetite among professionals for learning, for which there was no readily available product to fill the gap (Carswell, 2007; Watts, 2005).

There is no known amount, type or timing of alcohol that is safe in pregnancy and therefore the Scottish Chief Medical Officer's advice is to avoid alcohol when pregnant or trying to conceive (NHS Health Scotland, 2010). Alcohol use in Scotland is high with

Corresponding author:
Margaret Watts, Director of Public Health, NHS Western Isles, 37 South Beach Street, Stornoway, Isle of Lewis HS1 4BN, Scotland, UK.
Email: maggie.watts@nhs.net

alcohol sales of 11.2 litres of absolute alcohol for every adult over the age of 16 (NHS Health Scotland, 2013). Self-reported accounts of women's drinking indicate that more than 40% of those of reproductive age (16–44 years) exceed the recommended maximum daily and/or weekly consumption guidance (Scottish Government, 2014). This may place a large proportion of pregnancies at risk of alcohol exposure in utero, particularly in the early weeks when the foetus is developing rapidly and before the woman may know she is pregnant.

Although FASD is relatively more common in the offspring of women who are dependent on alcohol, the majority of cases occur in the children of women who have other drinking patterns including binge drinking. There are many other factors that help determine which children will be affected by maternal alcohol use, e.g. maternal nutritional status, genetic makeup, including how alcohol is metabolised, stress and deprivation.

Since FASD is not a condition that requires hospitalisation, it tends to be very difficult to identify the number of affected individuals. Other countries such as Canada, USA, France, South Africa and now Russia and Australia are considerably further ahead than the UK in recognition and it is considered that the worldwide incidence of FASD is around one per cent of live births. FASD is a lifelong and irreversible condition although early interventions are known to produce better outcomes (Streissguth, et al., 1996; Streissguth, et al., 2004).

Foetal Alcohol Syndrome (FAS) was recognised and named in the early 1970s and the first Scottish paper looking at a series of children born in the West of Scotland was published in 1981 (Beattie, et al., 1981; Beattie, Day and Cockburn, 1983).

The origins of action in Scotland

In Scotland there has been direct national action on addressing foetal alcohol harm since 2009. However, even before that time, a national target for alcohol screening and brief interventions in maternity services, although not formally connected to reducing the incidence of FASD, was beginning to have an impact in raising awareness of the frequency of alcohol use in pregnancy and the actions that could be taken to reduce consumption and harm.

In February 2009 the Scottish Framework on alcohol problems was published. This was built around challenging and changing the alcohol culture of Scotland and included actions to sustain alcohol brief interventions in maternity care (Scottish Government, 2009). Action 8 stated the commitment to arrange a survey of the incidence of FAS, the most readily recognised presentation of foetal alcohol harm. However, while the commitment had been made, there was no infrastructure through which this could be achieved. The first action that the Scottish Government took was to draw together a group of interested and knowledgeable professionals from across the health, education and social care sectors to discuss what a surveillance programme around FAS might look like. This group was supported by Professor Philip May, who has undertaken a number of prevalence studies on the occurrence of FASD in community and school populations. The conclusion drawn by that expert group was that the ideal scenario was a longitudinal cohort study of children born to mothers whose alcohol history was contemporaneously recorded and followed up. The group recognised that such a study would be at considerable expense with meticulous planning and take several years to provide any results. As such it was considered to be unfeasible to progress.

The Scottish FAS paediatric surveillance programme

Evidence has indicated that diagnosis before six years of age is of greatest benefit to the child (Streissguth, et al., 1996). Therefore, a small group of paediatricians involved in the stakeholder event developed and proposed to the Chief Scientist and Scottish Government that they undertake a passive surveillance study. The basis of this study was to use the database of the Royal College of Paediatrics and Child Health and the Scottish Paediatric Surveillance Unit to enquire of paediatricians in Scotland on a monthly basis whether they had seen a case of FAS in a child up to six years of age. Prior to the study's commencement, the investigators visited all major maternity and paediatric units in Scotland to talk to the paediatricians about the condition and the study. When a case was reported using the surveillance reporting form, the study's research nurse would follow up with the clinician to ensure that the case met with the case definition and to ascertain further details regarding maternal history and child presentation. The study began in January 2010 and was funded for four years.

Alongside this surveillance study, an annual awareness-raising conference was held, initially targeting paediatricians, health visitors and midwives but latterly extending to social work and education professionals.

Three-and-a-half years into the programme, by the time of the fourth conference the study had identified a steady but small number of cases of FAS totalling 37. This remains at a low level (approximately one-tenth of the prevalence anticipated based on worldwide research), but is in keeping with other international passive surveillance studies. The low level of reporting is considered to be due to a number of factors – a lack of familiarity with clinical presentation, a lack of reliable information about maternal drinking behaviours during pregnancy and a continuing low level of awareness of FAS among clinicians – in addition to the need for referral to paediatric services, where some children may not yet present a severe enough picture to warrant referral.

Scottish Government resources

Also starting in 2010, the Scottish Government took concerted action with the establishment of a small core team, based within maternal and child health rather than alcohol policy. The team's priorities focused on awareness-raising with professionals and wider aspects of prevention as providing the most effective approaches, and sought to work with the maternity services in engaging women with alcohol assessments in pregnancy and alcohol brief interventions.

E-learning module

As part of increasing the knowledge and awareness of professionals, NHS Education Scotland worked with the Scottish Government to commission an FASD interactive e-learning package. This was developed by Children in Scotland, a national voluntary sector agency with a special interest in FASD, together with SOFFED, a software company, resulting in an interactive, user-friendly resource. Using short presentations, video clips and quizzes to increase knowledge and understanding of the condition, this module provides a sound introduction and robust basis for learning about foetal alcohol harm.[2]

FASD Awareness Day toolkit

At the ninth hour on the ninth day of the ninth month, people around the world celebrate and remember International FASD Awareness Day. The day was selected to remind participants of the need to remain alcohol free for the nine-month duration of pregnancy. Drawing on an existing small pack developed by NHS Forth Valley and Forth Valley Alcohol and Drug Partnership, the Scottish Government (2013) produced an FASD Awareness Day electronic toolkit. This provides templates for media releases, quizzes, suggested activities and key messages around the theme of avoiding alcohol during pregnancy or when contemplating becoming pregnant. It is particularly aimed at health promotion teams who are seeking a resource to use to support their local FASD awareness-raising activities.

FASD training sessions

Following the development of the e-learning module and the FASD awareness day toolkit, and alongside the annual conference from the FAS surveillance programme, it became apparent that awareness among professionals of foetal alcohol harm has been rising. The Scottish Government considered that the low level of reporting in the surveillance programme could reflect poor confidence in recognising and diagnosing FAS, and that clinicians needed support and training to be able to identify, assess and diagnose accurately. In 2012, thanks to the award of a Winston Churchill Travelling Fellowship, the co-ordinator was able to visit the Manitoba FASD Centre in Winnipeg, and through this link the Scottish Government invited the Canadian team to Scotland to help move FASD work forward across the country. The Manitoba Centre recognises that multidisciplinary teams are best placed to assess and diagnose FASD and support the management of affected children and their families. Their approach involves paediatrics, clinical genetics, clinical psychology, speech and language therapy, occupational therapy and social work as core diagnostic disciplines. Each discipline is able to conduct an assessment of the strengths and challenges of the referred child specific to the discipline, and then participate in a multidisciplinary meeting to share and discuss the potential diagnosis and future management. For a diagnosis of FASD to be made, the maternal history of alcohol use must be confirmed.

The vision for bringing the Manitoba team to Scotland was to develop local teams of health and social care professionals who were capable and confident in assessing and diagnosing FASD, understood the strengths and challenges that the diagnosis may present for the affected child and their care givers, and could incorporate this work into their everyday practice. It was intended that local teams would be developed across Scotland, thereby increasing the availability of assessment and diagnostic capabilities.

A week-long training programme was set up for November 2013 with two days of health and social care professional training in Inverness repeated in Edinburgh, and one day set aside for caregivers of children and young people with FASD in Dunblane. Considerable effort was applied to gaining a good spread of health board team attendance and teams from nine of the 14 territorial NHS health boards took part. The training focused on providing the local teams – mainly comprising paediatrics, child and adolescent psychiatry, psychology (clinical and educational), speech and language therapy, occupational therapy and social work – with the tools to assess and identify children, conduct conversations with birth families and look at the next steps for their practice.

Initial evaluation immediately after the events showed that participants felt that their knowledge of FASD had increased and that the training had really 'hit the button' in terms of what they needed. The responses were highly positive and very encouraging. At the end of the second day for both sets of training was a session on 'Where next?' This allowed teams, together with their colleagues from different localities, to consider ways in which the training could be applied to practice in their areas and produced a number of positive suggestions to better identify and serve the needs of children with FASD. Follow-up of participants at three months demonstrated that some areas had begun to change how they were assessing and addressing children and families with suspected foetal alcohol harm.

The team from Manitoba reported being so impressed with the eagerness to learn and the enthusiasm and inquisitiveness of the delegates that they wished to come back in 18 months' time to see the progress that had been made.

Event for caregivers

Alongside the training for professionals, the Scottish Government wanted to be able to apply some of the knowledge developed by the Manitoba FASD Centre in supporting families and caregivers of children and young people with FASD. For too long, the needs of caregivers have been overlooked and their views been left unheard. The day in Dunblane allowed birth, foster and adoptive carers of children with FASD to come together, share their experiences and learn some strategies from the FASD Centre team, including the educationalist, about helping their children to maximise their strengths and overcome their challenges. The dedication of these caregivers and their willingness to enhance the care they provide was overwhelming.

Additional actions at local level

Some health board areas are taking further steps to address FASD through enhancing the contraception services for women of reproductive age. There is good evidence that effective contraception (including long-acting reversible methods such as hormonal implants or intrauterine contraceptive devices) can be of considerable value in reducing alcohol-exposed pregnancies (Floyd, et al., 2007; Peipert, et al., 2012). It is possible to provide training for addiction service nurses so that they can offer hormone implants as part of the holistic care of the woman with substance use problems, helping to increase her control over her life and moving her forwards on her recovery journey. Similarly, women attending sexual health and family planning services in some areas are beginning to be advised that when they wish to become pregnant they should cease their use of alcohol for the duration of the pregnancy.

Next steps

There is increasing evidence at health board level of a change in awareness around foetal alcohol harm and of more joined-up working and information exchange. To support this, a FASD Care Pathway is being developed which will cover babies and children up to secondary school age. The multi-agency multi-disciplinary group that is developing the care pathway is applying GIRFEC[3] principles to the work and engaging with health, education and social care professionals as well as the voluntary sector. The final product is intended to act as a decision support tool in determining appropriate courses of action to enhance the potential of the child, regardless of domestic circumstances.

Resourcing FASD work has been and remains a big issue. In the absence of a dedicated funding stream, making progress is a slow and rocky path and FASD remains the poor relation of similar sized neuro-behavioural congenital problems such as autistic spectrum disorder. I am hopeful that the work begun by Scottish Government will now be adopted by the health boards and local authorities who can work collaboratively to make a difference to the lives of the children and young people living daily with foetal alcohol harm.

Notes

1. Disclaimer: The views expressed in this article are those of the author and cannot be taken to be those of the Scottish Government or of NHS Western Isles.
2. The module can be found at www.knowledge.scot.nhs.uk/home/learning-and-cpd/learning-spaces/fasd.aspx.
3. The GIRFEC (Getting it Right for Every Child) approach supports practitioners across all services to focus on what makes a positive difference for children and young people – and how they can act to deliver these improvements (see www.gov.scot/resource/0042/00423979.pdf).

References

Beattie JO, Day RE and Cockburn F (1981) *Fetal Alcohol Syndrome: 40 cases from the West of Scotland.* Exeter: Pediatric Society.

Beattie JO, Day RE, Cockburn F and Garg RA (1983) Alcohol and the fetus in the West of Scotland. *British Medical Journal* 287: 17–20.

Carswell T (2007) Diagnosis of foetal alcohol syndrome in Scotland: a survey of paediatricians' knowledge, beliefs and practices. Submission for MPH thesis. University of Glasgow.

Floyd RJ, et al., and Project CHOICES Efficacy Study Group (2007) Preventing alcohol-exposed pregnancies: a randomized controlled trial. *American Journal of Preventative Medicine* 32(1): 1–10.

May P and Gossage JP (2001) Estimating the prevalence of fetal alcohol syndrome: a summary. *Alcohol Research and Health* 25(3): 159–166.

Mukherjee RAS, Wray E, Commers M, Hollins S and Curfs L (2013) The impact of raising a child with FASD upon carers: findings from a mixed methodology study in the UK. *Adoption & Fostering* 37(1): 43–56.

Mukherjee R, Wray E, Hollins S and Curfs L (2015) What does the general public in the UK know about the risk to a developing foetus if exposed to alcohol in pregnancy? Findings from a UK mixed methodology study. *Child: Care, Health and Development* 41: 467–474.

NHS Health Scotland (2010) Alcohol use: recommendations for pregnant women. Available at: www.maternal-and-early-years.org.uk/alcohol-use-recommendations-for-pregnant-women.

NHS Health Scotland (2013) Monitoring and evaluating Scotland's alcohol strategy: an update of alcohol sales and price band analyses. Available at: www.healthscotland.com/uploads/documents/21782-MESAS%20August%20Update%202013.pdf.

Peipert JF, Madden T, Allsworth JE and Secura GM (2012) Preventing unintended pregnancies by providing no-cost contraception. *Obstetrics & Gynecology* 120(6): 1291–1297.

Scottish Government (2009) *Changing Scotland's Relationship with Alcohol: A framework for action.* Available at: www.gov.scot/Resource/Doc/262905/0078610.pdf.

Scottish Government (2013) *Fetal Alcohol Spectrum Disorder Toolkit.* Available at: www.scotland.gov.uk/Publications/2013/10/3881.

Scottish Government (2014) The Scottish Health Survey 2013. Available at: www.gov.scot/Publications/2014/12/9982/0.

Streissguth AP, Barr HM, Kogan J and Bookstein FL (1996) *Final Report: Understanding the occurrence of secondary disabilities in clients with fetal alcohol syndrome (FAS) and fetal alcohol effects (FAE).* Seattle, WA: University of Washington Publication Services.

Streissguth AP, Bookstein FL, Barr HM, Sampson PD, O'Malley K and Young JK (2004) Risk factors for adverse life outcomes in fetal alcohol syndrome and fetal alcohol effects. *Journal of Developmental & Behavioral Pediatrics* 25(4): 228–238.

Watts M (2005) Services for children with fetal alcohol syndrome in Ayrshire & Arran. Submission for membership of the Faculty of Public Health.

Dr Margaret Watts is Director of Public Health, NHS Western Isles, Stornoway, Isle of Lewis HS1 2BN, Scotland, UK.

adoption
&fostering

Adoption & Fostering
2015, Vol. 39(3) 263–269

DOI: 10.1177/0308575915603300
adoptionfostering.sagepub.com
SAGE

England and Wales

Non-agency intercountry adoption

In the Matter of S and T (Children) [2015] Family Court at the RCJ Munby P 19 June 2015 [2015] EWHC 1753 (Fam)

Two girls, now aged three and two-and-a-half, were born of Pakistani parents who separated at the end of 2012 when the father took them back to Pakistan against the mother's wishes. The children were made wards of court in January 2013 and returned to the UK with their father remaining in Pakistan. The family decided that the most appropriate long-term carers for the children were a great aunt and uncle who lived in Illinois. They issued an application for residence orders and leave to remove the children from the jurisdiction. In the meantime the girls were cared for by an uncle in Reading. The family then discovered that US immigration law would require the children to be adopted in accordance with the Hague Convention on Intercountry Adoption before they would be able to live permanently in the USA. The father applied to take the children back to Pakistan to live with him (they remained wards of court as a result of the order made in 2013).

While proceedings continued, the court made repeated orders allowing the children to go to the USA for periods of 90 days, that being the longest permitted by holiday visas, and declared that the children remained habitually resident in England and Wales. The local authority for the area in which the children were living was asked to consider taking the children into care, and making an agency placement of the children with their relatives in the USA. They concluded that this was not appropriate, as the children were not at any risk of harm which would justify an application for a care order and their father, despite some difficulties, was willing and able to care for them himself.

The relatives in the USA were ineligible to apply for an adoption order in England, as they did not fulfil the habitual residence or domicile requirements of section 50 of the Adoption and Children Act 2002. They applied for parental responsibility for the children prior to adoption abroad under section 84 of the Act. The Adoptions with a Foreign Element Regulations 2005 provide for various sections of the Act setting out requirements for adoption to apply in the case of applications under section 84. These include the requirement to give notice to the prescribed local authority. The prescribed local authority is either the local authority in which the applicants have their home at the time of making the application, or, where they no longer have a home in the area of an English or Welsh local authority, the local one in which they last had a home (in various permutations set out in the Local Authority (Adoption) (Miscellaneous Provisions) Regulations 2005).

The applicants had never lived in the UK and therefore could not identify a prescribed local authority. They gave notice to Reading

Borough Council as the area in which the children last had a home, but the court ruled that this was irrelevant and had no effect. The President also considered the requirement in section 42(7)(b) that an order cannot be made unless the court is satisfied that sufficient opportunity to observe the child and applicants in the home environment has been afforded to the local authority within whose area the home is. The President referred to *Re A (Adoption: Removal)* [2009] EWCA Civ 41, where the Court of Appeal considered the case of a child placed with relatives overseas by an adoption agency. It established that where section 42(7)(a) applied (placement by an agency), there was no requirement that the home environment had to be within England and Wales. In that case the Court of Appeal had also considered section 47(7)(b) and concluded that it was plain that where the child had not been placed by an agency, the home had to be in the area of a UK local authority.

The father did not consent to the proposed adoption and argued that as the Convention required that the persons giving the necessary consent to adoption did so freely, it was not open to the court to dispense with his consent. The President did not accept this argument, as the Regulations made it clear that section 52 (dispensing with consent) applies to applications under section 84; if the court decided that the father's consent should be dispensed with, his consent would no longer be necessary under the Convention. The President did accept that there would need to be further examination of how the Hague Convention processes would apply if a parent's consent had been dispensed with, but did not believe that it would be impossible.

In considering whether to dispense with the father's consent, the President applied the *Re B-S* test of whether 'nothing else will do'. He accepted that some of the father's actions (removing the children to Pakistan, not being involved with the children for a year and forging documents from the mother) were 'deplorable'. The children's guardian did not recommend placement of the children with the father, feeling that although if there was no other option, the father could be good enough, the children would be better placed with their mother's family. The President quoted from *Y v UK* [2012] 55 EHRR 33: 'It is not enough to show that a child could be placed in a more beneficial environment for his upbringing.'

Held

Although a section 84 order could be made by dispensing with parental consent, in this case the children's welfare did not require it, as the father would be able to care adequately for the children. Even if consent had been dispensed with, the applicants would have to establish a home, however temporary, in the area of a British local authority before an order could be made. The application was dismissed.

Adoption application: leave to oppose

Re LG (A child) [2015]
Family Court at the RCJ Baker J
22 June 2015 [2015] EWFC 52

L was born in March 2014 to young parents whose relationship had broken down before her birth. A mother and baby foster placement broke down after a few days and the child was accommodated by the local authority. The local authority started care proceedings and in August 2014 final care and placement orders were made. The parents had failed to identify anybody within their family who might be able to care for L and the father had repeatedly refused to allow his family to be told about L's birth. He claimed that he had suffered an abusive childhood at the hands of his own father and did not want them to be involved. The father disengaged from contact before the final hearing and the mother had a final visit in September, shortly before the child was placed with prospective adopters. In December 2014, the father told his family about L and they immediately approached the local authority wanting to care for her. In January 2015, the adopters filed their application to adopt L and the father applied for permission to oppose the application on the basis of a change in circumstances. Directions were given for viability assessment of three paternal family members, followed by a full special guardianship assessment of the most appropriate relative. All viability assessments were positive, as was the full Special Guardianship Order (SGO) assessment of the proposed carer, the paternal grandfather.

The court held that the application for the father to oppose the adoption was the appropriate one to make, despite the fact that he had caused the situation by lying about his childhood and refusing to involve his family. The adopters argued that this was not a father applying because of a change in circumstances, but an application 'by the back door' by the grandfather, who did not fall within the class of persons able to apply to oppose under section 47(5). They argued that the court should treat this as an application for leave to make an SGO application and therefore that the judge should not be restricted by the welfare checklist in section 1. They argued that if the court allowed an application to remove a child from a settled and successful adoption placement, there would be considerable policy consequences. Prospective adopters would be discouraged from coming forward because of the risk of attachment to a child who might later be removed, and those who had a child placed might refrain from applying for an adoption order for several years in the hope that the court would be less likely to contemplate removing the child.

The court declined to follow this route and considered only the welfare of L in coming to their decision, applying the *Re B-S* test of whether 'nothing else [but adoption] would do'. Although L had been settled with the adopters for eight months and was likely to suffer emotional distress from being moved to live with a family she did not know, this was not a factor that would override her welfare requirement of being brought up within her birth family.

Held

The father was granted leave to oppose the adoption order. After taking advice the adopters withdrew their adoption application and L moved quickly to live with her grandfather.

Comment

The judge expressed the hope that this judgement would not deter future adopters from putting themselves forward. He emphasised that this case was very unusual, but that adopters must be aware that the law allows applications for leave to be made, albeit that they will be made in a minority of cases and most applications will not succeed. *A and B v Rotherham Metropolitan Borough Council* [2014] EWFC 47 was the first reported case of a child being removed from a settled placement with prospective adopters and placed with a family carer (as a result of the mother identifying the wrong man as the father and the real father not coming forward until after the child had been placed). Holman J in that case said that he had 'rarely heard a more harrowing case'; the child was placed with 'perfect adopters' and had settled well, but his long-term welfare required that he move to paternal family that he had never met. It must be concerning that a case described as unusual and fact specific should be followed so swiftly by another having the same harrowing effect. Does this mean that the courts are now more willing to consider removing children from prospective adopters or is this a co-incidence? Will adopters be prepared to take the apparently real risk of a child returning to birth family after settling into their 'forever family'? We have no real idea of how the children will be affected by such a move or whether social workers should somehow build the risk of such a decision into their preparation of a child for a permanent placement.

In this case the judge emphasised the need for a local authority to identify family members at an early stage and not to be easily distracted by parents who may conceal the truth. We have case law (*Re C v XYZ County Council* [2007] EWCA Civ 1206) which requires a local authority to critically examine information given by a birth mother relinquishing her child as to why she does not want her family told about the child, but there is no absolute requirement for an adoption agency to inform the birth family if to do so would cause delay in the child's placement. It would be helpful for guidance to be given to assist local authorities in deciding just how far they should go in care cases to investigate potential birth family placements against the parents' express wishes and to what extent they should be able to breach the parents' right to privacy in the possible interests of a family placement for the child.

Alexandra Conroy Harris, Legal Consultant (England), BAAF, prepared these notes.

Northern Ireland

The Children (Northern Ireland) Order 1995: Article 50(2), care proceedings; threshold criteria and parental fault

In the Matter of M (A child) (Threshold criteria – terminal illness)
The High Court, O'Hara J
27 May 2015

Background

This case concerned Mrs B (in her early 40s) and her son M (aged 4). The identity of M's father was unknown: Ms B declined to disclose his name but asserted that he had died of a drugs overdose after M was born. Ms B has a mild learning disability and lived in foster care from the age of 5 to 18, after which she spent some time living in supported accommodation before being admitted to a psychiatric hospital following an overdose. She remained there for approximately six years before moving to supported living accommodation and then to semi-independent living. In 2010 she became pregnant, was diagnosed with breast cancer and had a mastectomy.

After M's birth early in 2011, Ms B was able to care for him with support from the Trust. This was successful to the extent that M's name was removed from the Child Protection Register late in 2011. In 2013, M was assessed as having general developmental delay, with a possibility of having a long-term learning disability and speech problems. All of this led to M becoming a looked after child but remaining in the care of his mother.

At a Looked After Children meeting in 2014 it was apparent that Ms B's health, which had been problematic for some time, was deteriorating and with her agreement M was voluntarily accommodated while she went for tests. Within a very short time she was diagnosed with terminal cancer. Since then the Trust has sought unsuccessfully to identify a family member or a friend who can look after M in the long term. M has stayed with carers since June 2014. He still sees his mother but that contact has become less frequent, in part because she does not want him to be distressed by her appearance.

The Trust issued care proceedings in December 2014, due to its concern that no one would have parental responsibility for M, and Ms B agreed to interim care orders being made. However, in February 2015 she stated that she did not want any long-term care plan for M to include adoption 'as I am concerned about his name potentially being changed and him forgetting about me as his mother'. She added that she was fully committed to having as much contact as she could with M, depending on her health.

O'Hara J noted a complicating feature which had emerged was that Ms B had appointed a testamentary guardian, a Ms A with whom she had developed a friendship. Ms A had considered whether she could foster or adopt M and concluded that she could not but appreciated that as M's testamentary guardian she would have parental responsibility for him after Ms B's death. She would like to play a role in any decisions to be made about his life, for example, to ensure that he is placed with suitable foster carers and receives the religious sacraments. She envisages herself acting like an aunt to M but with the possibility of reconsidering the extent of her role if any change in her work commitments made that possible.

Submissions

Counsel for the Trust emphasised that it did not and never had suggested that the issues about M's future care represented any attribution of fault to Ms B. She suggested that the emergence of Ms A's position as a testamentary guardian did not fundamentally alter the position, which was that M was a four-year-old boy, with an entirely uncertain present and future, at risk of coming to significant harm. She then stated the statutory grounds for making a care order as set out in Article 50(2) of the 1995 Children's Order. She submitted that:

> ...without it being anybody's fault, Ms B cannot care for her son as a result of her terminal ill-health and her combination of illnesses...further, it does not matter at what date threshold criteria are assessed. In June 2014, Ms B placed M in voluntary accommodation without an interim care order when she was too unwell to care for M. At that date she did not know that she was dying. Later in December 2014 when the Trust issued care proceedings, Ms B was still too unwell to care for him but did know that she was dying. In her February 2015 statement Ms B said that she could no longer care for M on a daily basis. That statement is correct but also reflects the true position from June 2014 onwards.

She asserted that the threshold criteria were satisfied because: M is a four-year-old child who is likely to suffer significant harm due to the care being given to him and likely to be given to him if the order were not made, not being what it would be reasonable to expect a parent to give; M's needs as a result of his known and possible level of disability are such that he needs additional care and support; and apart from Ms B, who cannot provide the care that M needs, there is no other person who can provide such care.

Counsel for Ms B submitted that the Trust's application was misconceived because it was based on the misconception that nobody would have parental responsibility for M after his client's death, whereas Ms A would in fact have that responsibility as his testamentary guardian. He further contended that Ms B was currently capable of exercising parental responsibility because she was able to make decisions about M's welfare. He drew attention to the judgement of Thorpe J in *Birmingham City Council v. D; Birmingham City Council v. M*,[1] which involved two different sets of children: in one family the mother had died and the unmarried father declined any responsibility for the children; in the other family both parents were dead. The public authority which was accommodating the children applied for care orders, concerned that nobody held parental responsibility for them. In finding that the threshold criteria could not be satisfied, the judge held that 'it would be a plain distortion of the threshold test to find some theoretical risk of harm when none in reality is discernible'. The care order provisions were not applicable.

Counsel for the guardian ad litem initially submitted that the Trust was on the wrong track by seeking a care order when it should be applying for leave under Article 173 of the 1995 Order to pursue wardship. However, the guardian later reconsidered her position to endorse the Trust's approach, accepting that culpability is not necessary for threshold criteria to be established and because the Trust's exercise of its duties to promote the welfare of M was not sufficient protection for him. This drew from O'Hara J the comment that:

> Article 173 provides that the court retains its inherent jurisdiction to make children wards of court. However, that power is not to be exercised unless the court is satisfied that the result could not be achieved other than through the exercise of the inherent jurisdiction.

Discussion

O'Hara J indicated that the real issue was the care plan – long-term foster care or adoption – but that was a matter for future debate. At this stage, the court was considering only whether the threshold criteria had been established. Noting that the statutory requirements for a care order are not couched in terms of fault – that was not a prerequisite for the making of orders – he drew attention to *Re B (A child)*[2] in which Lady Hale (at para 191) had stated:

> The harm, or the likelihood of harm, must be 'attributable to the care given to the child or likely to be given to him if an order were not made, not being what it would be reasonable to expect a parent to give to him'... This reinforces the view that it is a deficiency in parental *care* rather than in parental *character*, which must cause the harm. It also means that the court should be able to identify what that deficiency in care might be and how likely it is to happen.

Rejecting the contention of counsel for Ms B that the decision of Thorpe J could be applied to the present case by analogy, O'Hara J instead found that 'the tragic fact is that M is only being protected from inevitable harm, namely the impairment of his health or development, because of the Trust's intervention in June 2014... the only real difference between her condition in June 2014 and her condition from July 2014 is that her condition had been diagnosed by the later date'. He was therefore satisfied that the Trust had established the threshold criteria and on that basis the case could proceed to final hearing, adding: 'It does not follow from threshold criteria being established that a care order will necessarily be made and there are obvious issues to be considered about whether long-term foster care or adoption is to be preferred.'

O'Hara J concluded by referring back to the reasons given by Ms B for opposing the adoption of M – that his name might be changed and that he would forget about her as his mother. On the first issue, O'Hara J acknowledged that adoption would be more likely lead to a change in his name than would be the case if he remained in long-term foster care; on the second he took the view that 'there is little difference between the two options. Whether and for how long M will remember Ms B may be affected by the extent of his developmental delay and any disability which emerges.' However, he considered it obvious that 'a life story record must be prepared so that as M's life continues he can be informed about his background. That is what happens in most cases and there are powerful reasons for it being done here.' He suggested that 'it would require little effort or imagination to devise a role in M's future for Ms A through whom an appropriate and supportive memory of Ms B could be maintained'. Finally, he paid tribute to the Trust's long and positive record of working with Ms B to help her and her son, noting that its application to the court had been made with the best of intentions and concluded: 'It would be disappointing if a way could not be found through the differences between it and Ms B at this late stage of her life.'

Held

Trust application granted.

Comment

The critical fact is that the only surviving parent, seemingly with no relatives, is dying leaving her four-year-old child with no one who can legally undertake parental responsibility. An ancillary fact is that he has 'been with carers' for the past 10 months. The probability is that the Trust is working towards adoption as the preferred care plan; which in the circumstances, as far as they are known, cannot be faulted. It would have been interesting to have had more exploration of just how the facts in this case could be distinguished from those that led Thorpe J to take an alternative decision; given the availability of statuory options, wardship was a red herring; and the testamentary appointment, while offering a positive opportunity for an ongoing bridge in this child's life, did not address the fundamental issue of legal responsibility.

It does seem an awful burden for this faultless mother to have to endure at this tragic time but perhaps if she can have confidence in the arrangements being made, and the people involved, it will make things slightly easier.

Kerry O'Halloran, lawyer, social worker and Adjunct Professor, Centre of Philanthropy and Non-profit Studies, QUT, Brisbane, Australia, prepared these notes.

Notes

1. [1994] 2 FLR 502
2. [2013] UKSC 33

The problems of making a diagnosis of FAS/FASD in the neonatal period

Adoption & Fostering
2015, Vol. 39(3) 270–274

DOI: 10.1177/0308575915598939
adoptionfostering.sagepub.com

Introduction

Foetal alcohol syndrome (FAS) was first described in the early 1970s and for a long time was thought to be a syndrome which you either 'had' or 'didn't have'. Since that time, and particularly over the last 20 years, it has become clearer that there is a spectrum of problems that babies and children can develop as a consequence of foetal alcohol exposure. Furthermore, not all of the features (including the classical facial features originally described) necessarily need to be present, and children can be affected in different ways within the complicated facets of child development. Different diagnostic labels have been used over time including terms such as 'foetal alcohol effects', 'partial FAS' and 'alcohol-related neurodevelopmental disorder'. Detailed discussion of this aspect is beyond the scope of these notes, and therefore the umbrella term foetal alcohol spectrum disorders (FASD) has been used to describe the whole spectrum of those who may be affected as a consequence of foetal alcohol exposure, with FAS lying at the most severe end of this spectrum.

There are a number of very good reasons for attempting to make a diagnosis of FAS/FASD as soon as possible. Above all, making the correct diagnosis can ensure that the right management and support are in place to secure the best outcome for the child, and there is evidence that this can improve outcome. Additionally, the risk of having an affected child rises with maternal age and with each pregnancy, and therefore recognition raises the possibility of intervention to prevent further children from being affected.

The shortened timescale in place in the UK since 2014 with respect to legal proceedings places further pressure on the need to make a correct diagnosis at an early stage where care orders are required. Undiagnosed FAS/FASD is thought to be a common cause of adoptive placement breakdown (Phillips, 2007).

Finally, if foetal alcohol exposure during pregnancy has not been recognised, it can be almost impossible to trace an accurate pregnancy history to assess exposure many years later.

What is needed to make a diagnosis?

Foetal alcohol exposure is clearly a prerequisite to be able to make a diagnosis of FAS/FASD (although there are sometimes occasions where this is unknown and has to assumed in retrospect). In addition to such exposure, three further aspects are required to make a diagnosis of FAS (also see Gregory, this journal):

(1) poor growth (this may be prenatal and/or postnatal);

(2) typical facial features (classical triad of small palpebral fissures, smooth philtrum and thin top lip);
(3) nervous system abnormality (structural or functional).

When all of these features are present, it is possible to make a diagnosis of FAS. If some, but not all of them are apparent then, in the context of prenatal alcohol exposure, a diagnosis of FASD needs to be considered. The third possibility is that there has been foetal alcohol exposure at a level which has raised concern, but the infant displays none of the above. There are potential difficulties with the definitions regarding each feature, considered separately below.

Poor growth

The problem here is that many factors can affect foetal growth adversely. The term small for gestational age (SGA) can be applied to babies whose weight is less than the 10th centile for their gestational age (intra-uterine growth restriction or IUGR is also commonly used to mean the same thing). This factor is a relatively poor discriminator as 10% of all babies will fall within this description by definition. As well as babies who are smaller than they might otherwise have been, this group will include some who are small but normal, and will exclude infants who weigh greater than the 10th centile, but are still smaller than they would otherwise have been without any adverse intra-uterine factors. Sometimes serial antenatal scans can be helpful in trying to determine the factors involved in poor antenatal growth.

Maternal illness or ill-health (including poor nutrition), smoking, substance misuse and complications of pregnancy, such as pregnancy-induced hypertension and pre-eclampsia, are among the causes of poor intra-uterine growth. These factors should be taken into account when evaluating the reasons why a baby might be smaller than expected. In a mother who is drinking alcohol during pregnancy, if there are no other discernible antenatal factors, then a baby who is SGA is much more likely to be small as a consequence of the maternal alcohol intake; the reality, however, is often confusing with multiple factors involved.

Choosing a lower centile threshold such as the 3rd centile will increase the chances of picking babies who are truly affected, but increase the likelihood of missing those who are affected more mildly, i.e. higher sensitivity but lower specificity.

Once the adverse antenatal factors are removed, one might expect that growth of the newborn baby would improve and continue at the genetic potential, and this is indeed often the case when growth impairment has been due to the consequences of placental insufficiency. In some cases when there has been significant foetal alcohol exposure, postnatal growth remains impaired. It is the author's experience that significantly affected babies (less than 0.4th centile) often have poor appetites and difficulties with feeding and swallowing co-ordination. This can contribute to reduced energy intake, but when this is corrected with either a high energy formula or nasogastric tube feeding, growth still remains poor.

Facial features

The classical triad of facial features is well described and is almost unique to foetal alcohol exposure. (Foetal hydantion syndrome (phenytoin exposure) and maternal phenylketonuria can be relatively easily excluded from the history.) These features are the size of palpebral fissures (from the endocanthion to the exocanthion of each eye), the smoothness of the philtrum and the thinness of the top lip. It can be useful to use structured scales demonstrating the full range of facial features and including racial variants (FAS Diagnostic and Prevention Network, undated) but these images do not cover the newborn period. Software is also available to assess facial features using digital photographs from the same source, but does not contain ranges well validated in the newborn period. Furthermore, taking good-quality images in this age group is challenging, so assessment often remains subjective. The face also changes in shape from infancy through to adolescence and adulthood, and the longitudinal progress of these changes is not well documented.

Nervous system abnormality

Problems with the nervous system can be structural or functional. One abnormality that has been described in association with foetal alcohol exposure is agenesis of the corpus callosum, the structure in the middle of the brain that acts as a 'bridge' between the two cerebral hemispheres. Other abnormalities can occur but in general an anatomical abnormality is unusual even in the context of documented heavy alcohol consumption. An ultrasound of the newborn brain is an easy-to-perform, non-invasive test that can help to document the presence or absence of an abnormality, and could be performed in all babies considered to be at risk. Other more complicated imaging modalities such as MRI show the myelination of the nervous pathways in addition to structural information, but may be better left until the child is at least one to two years of age or older when the brain is more mature.

Brain size is clearly important (and palpebral fissure measurement may be a proxy for this) and antenatal alcohol exposure can affect brain growth in the foetus. The head circumference at birth can be affected by the 'moulding' at delivery through the birth canal, but this usually resolves within a few days. If the head circumference measurement is less than the 10th centile, this may indicate that the brain growth is reduced, but there are problems if this observation is over-interpreted for the same reasons as birth weight. If a foetus has intrauterine growth restriction as a result of nutritional deprivation, the body weight centile is usually reduced compared with the head circumference centile. This is often called 'head-sparing' and reflects the foetus deflecting blood supply and nutrition to the most vital organs. What is especially concerning in terms of alcohol exposure is when the head circumference centile is below the body weight and length centiles. One might have increasing levels of concern with smaller head circumference centiles – particularly below the 2nd centile.

I have observed significant feeding dysfunction in some babies exposed to high levels of foetal alcohol exposure. This may be a manifestation of more general or later neurological dysfunction.

Of course the nub of the problem here is the 'not yet' – those infants who are going to develop neuro-behavioural or psychiatric problems later, of which we are unaware at the present time. In this situation the background history may not be relevant until a much later date when these problems can be given their appropriate context. Of course, many children may have been on course to develop some of these difficulties even without foetal alcohol exposure, and therein lies the diagnostic difficulty for community paediatricians and child and learning disability psychiatrists. Evidence from North America suggests that the right early support and interventions appropriate for FASD improve outcome, reinforcing the need for the context and the appropriate diagnostic label.

Foetal alcohol exposure: how much is too much?

The short answer to this seemingly simple question is that it is not possible to accurately determine the risk of an individual baby developing signs of future neuro-developmental impairment, nor even accurately predict the type of impairment. The 'higher the level of foetal alcohol exposure, the higher the risk' makes sense as an intellectual construct that is difficult to argue against from a biological standpoint, and so far, no research has been able to determine a threshold or safe limit. But how does one assess what is a significant level of foetal exposure, and therefore at a practical level determine which babies may benefit from further follow-up and developmental surveillance to detect future abnormalities?

Our own local figures suggest that around 20% of women continue to drink alcohol in some way during pregnancy and this information is similar to a study in Stafford and the Growing Up in Ireland Study (Layte and McCrory, 2014; Staffordshire County Council, 2014). However, to follow up one in five babies does not seem practical or realistic. At least half of all pregnancies are unplanned and therefore it is common for women to continue drinking without being aware that they may be pregnant – even up to what may subsequently turn out to be six to eight weeks of pregnancy. Our own data (anonymous lifestyle questionnaire) suggest that around four to five per cent of women continue to drink three to 14 units per week as pregnancy progresses.

Practical advice

My own personal practice is to refer babies for ongoing developmental surveillance when there is possible evidence of any of the following: growth impairment which may be related to foetal alcohol exposure, affected facial features and neurological impairment. I also refer babies for continuing developmental surveillance where there have been high levels of continuing alcohol use throughout the second or third trimesters or evidence of continuing 'binges'.

If there have been early alcohol binges during the first trimester or early regular alcohol use which responded to intervention, subsequent foetal growth is normal, as is newborn assessment, then I simply write to the GP, health visitor and community paediatricians to document what has happened, and to provide a background context in case problems develop later in childhood.

Conclusion

These notes have highlighted the difficulties associated with assessment of the newborn infant in the context of foetal alcohol exposure. There are difficulties in making an assessment in the newborn period and in trying to predict the future outcome for any infant. Differences in levels and timing of alcohol exposure, genetic susceptibility and metabolism may account for many of these differences.

Clearly there are important reasons, which have been highlighted, to make an accurate and timely diagnosis, but these laudable aims are restricted by the need to allow the developing nervous system to mature before understanding how children may subsequently be affected – particularly in ways that depend upon more sophisticated and complicated function and therefore only present in late childhood or early adolescence. It is the developmental outcome which is ultimately the most important, but about which we have the least idea at birth.

It is possible to identify children at birth who may be at the more severely affected end of the spectrum, but for many it will be a case of just identifying children who may be at particular risk and highlighting those who may merit developmental surveillance. One might expect that babies who have abnormal growth and/or facial features are more likely to develop future neurological abnormalities.

Many professionals find the diagnosis of FASD difficult for several of the reasons put forward here as well as others, and charities and support groups have played an important part in helping and supporting parents and professionals with diagnosis and interventions in this heterogeneous – and often poorly understood – disorder.

References

FAS Diagnostic and Prevention Network (undated) *Lip-philtrum guides*. Seattle, WA: University of Washington. Available at: http://depts.washington.edu/fasdpn/htmls/lip-philtrum-guides.htm.

Layte R and McCrory C (2014) *Growing up in Ireland study: maternal health behaviours and child growth in infancy*. Available at: www.growingup.ie/fileadmin/user_upload/documents/Maternal_Health_Report/GUI_Infant_Maternal_Health_4_web.pdf.

Phillips R (ed.) (2007) *Children Exposed to Parental Substance Misuse*, 3rd edn. London: BAAF.

Staffordshire County Council (2014) *Reducing alcohol-related harm: everyone's responsibility*. Available at: www.staffordshire.gov.uk/health/PublicHealth/Annual-Public-Health-Report-2013.pdf.

Dr Neil Aiton, Consultant Neonatologist, Brighton & Sussex University NHS Trust, prepared these notes.

adoption & fostering

Book reviews

Adoption & Fostering
2015, Vol. 39(3) 275–279

DOI: 10.1177/0308575915602584
adoptionfostering.sagepub.com

Foetal Alcohol Spectrum Disorders: Parenting a child with an invisible disability by Julia Brown and Dr Mary Mather. Oxford: FASD Trust (2014) (www.fasdtrust.co.uk) 152 pages. £7.99. ISBN 978 1 500851 88 0

Reviewed by Rena Phillips, Independent Practitioner, Co-ordinator, Post Adoption Central Support (PACS), Scotland, UK

In 2004 I edited a book for BAAF titled *Children Exposed to Parental Substance Misuse: Implications for family placement* (Phillips, 2004), where the effects of drinking during pregnancy were discussed. A decade later, I am struck by the increasing magnitude and seriousness of FASD and the extent to which it is repressed by society. Crucially, there is a lack of knowledge and understanding of the subject by social work, health and education professionals. A colleague who is a clinical psychologist referred to the condition as a ticking time bomb – it is not out of place to say that it has exploded.

There is only one published piece of UK research on the experiences and needs of carers of children with FASD (Mukherjee et al., 2013). It concludes that they feel unsupported and blamed for poor parenting. I am a member of adoption and foster care panels and co-ordinator of a post-adoption support service in central Scotland. My reading of the BAAF Form E on children registered for permanence indicates that social workers under-respond to alcohol misuse as compared to drug misuse and, importantly, fail to get the accurate alcohol history that is often denied by the birth mother. Prospective substitute families thus miss out on reliable information, advice and guidance to help them parent an affected child. More alarming, some families are parenting in the dark having taken on children without being told about possible alcohol brain damage. They struggle to access specialist services that are vital to placing disabled children successfully. This book is therefore very welcome.

The authors offer a good combination of medical expertise and direct practical experience. The book is described as intended for parents and carers, for whom it provides an empowering and supportive resource, but it is equally essential reading for social work, health and education professionals, as well as extended family members and friends. Although FASD is a complex and at times confusing subject, it is presented here in a clear and accessible style. The chapters are brief, convenient for busy families and professionals and easy to dip in and out of. The authors offer a great deal of advice and guidance, referred to as strategies rather than solutions.

The cover features a somewhat bewildered octopus. Its tentacles represent the maze of multiple diagnoses that families can find themselves embroiled in, with resulting conflicting explanations and advice. As there is no one test for FASD, it is recommended practice that an assessment leading to a diagnosis is carried out by a multidisciplinary team. The Scottish

Government put out information on the availability of such teams in Health Boards in Scotland. I spent some time searching for this to be eventually told they did not exist. As the book indicates, it can still be very difficult for parents to find a doctor who is prepared to diagnose FASD. This not only requires professional knowledge and support but also action at government and policy level. The UK is clearly disadvantaged by a lack of political will to resource such work.

The book begins by looking at the unpredictable impact of alcohol on the developing brain and its lifelong influence. Mary Mather consistently advocates for carers to have a comprehensive birth family medical history, as well as a personal child medical history, and this is strongly emphasised in her chapter on FASD in relation to adoption and foster care. The core of the text deals with what does and does not work in parenting children with FASD and why. Traditional behaviour strategies such as time out, grounding, money as a reward and talking therapies are deemed unsuccessful. General strategies that can help include consistency in daily routine, a structured environment, constant high level of supervision and the building up of a local network of support for the future. Later chapters offer ideas for tackling more specific behavioural issues such as hypersensitivity to touch, light and sound, eating and sleeping difficulties, aggression and the management of discipline. The section about communication is particularly relevant from an assessment perspective. As Julia Brown reiterates elsewhere in this journal, affected children are described as chatty, but are behind with spoken language: 'This difficulty with understanding and processing information which is given verbally is at the heart of the massive frustration felt by carers, teachers and others. How can this apparently bright, intelligent, chatty child not follow and obey a simple adult-led instruction?' (p.79). The concluding chapters on growing up with disability focus on education and the transition to adolescence in relation to issues such as independence, arrested social development and friendships.

I was interested in the guidance offered in the book to 'own the diagnosis'; it is advised that the earlier affected children know and understand in age-appropriate ways about FASD, the more positive are the outcomes for them as adults. This subject encompasses potential painful and distressing themes around identity, difference and stigma that merit further exploration.

Some children would have experienced the double jeopardy of being exposed to alcohol damage before birth and of remaining with birth parents incapacitated by their continued substance misuse. Those separated from their birth families will experience loss and guilt. The move to a substitute permanent family could trigger the question of whether they were adopted because of their disability. Their need to understand the past can be hampered by a lack of full background information, including medical information in relation to FASD. For some, a sensitive issue will be the fact that their impairment was caused by their birth mother, which can generate distressed and angry feelings. This poses extra challenges when there is post-placement contact with birth families. Such vulnerabilities will require responsive and skilled intervention to help children affected by FASD to obtain a clear and positive sense of personal identity.

This small volume packs in an impressive amount of advice and guidance. An adoptive parent whose opinion I sought remarked that while this was very positive, it could be experienced as too prescriptive. Nevertheless, the impressive spirit of the book is that it promotes the individuality of affected children, stressing there is no right or wrong way to parent them. It very much seeks to hold on to the potential and strengths of affected children as well as those of their parents and carers, and it does so in a loving and sympathetic way. Needless to say, it is highly recommended.

References

Mukherjee R, Wray E, Commers M, Hollins S and Curfs L (2013) The impact of raising a child with FASD upon carers: findings from a mixed methodology study in the UK. *Adoption & Fostering* 37(3): 43–56.

Phillips R (2004) *Children Exposed to Parental Substance Misuse: Implications for family placement*. London: BAAF.

Assessing Disorganized Attachment Behaviour in Children by David Shemmings and Yvonne Shemmings (eds) London: Jessica Kingsley Publishers (2014) 240 pages. £22.99. ISBN 978 1 849053 22 8

Reviewed by Stuart Harragan, Family and Network Practitioner, The Mulberry Bush Specialist Residential School for Traumatised Children, Oxfordshire, UK

Over the course of the last ten years or so, there has been a significant development in the broad understanding of attachment theory and its relevance to work with children and families. In my experience of working in therapeutic communities, this has come as a relief accompanied by some frustration. Professionals' knowledge of the field can range from a broad overview to an in-depth, sophisticated understanding. During the last decade I cannot recall encountering a single social worker who does not at least give a nod of acknowledgement when the subject is mentioned in relation to a child for whom they are responsible. However, clumsy application of the theory can be harmful, such as when the term 'attachment disorder' is used haphazardly and becomes an assumption rather than a formal diagnosis. This can prove unhelpful when considering the next appropriate course of professional intervention for the child and family.

The purpose of this book is to describe the ADAM Project Pathway Model and how the five tools that form part of it can be used to assess children's behaviour. This commences after a helpful and clear summary of Bowlby and Ainsworth's work, also acknowledging the cautions described above. In the second chapter, the skills needed to help families post assessment are specified in simple terms, such as using empathic responses to open up dialogue and maintaining a stance of 'non-directive curiosity' by suspending annoyance and incredulity, as well as being non-judgemental – social work basics one might imagine, but the reality of a busy children and families team can easily cause these skills to be lost. Moreover, the method is not one to be used in isolation as the benefits of team working and the 'right kind' of supervision are highlighted.

From the beginning, the authors make it absolutely clear that despite the varied and evidence-based tools provided, the aim is to identify *disorganised attachment behaviour* and not to furnish anyone with the authority to make a formal diagnosis. This distinction is vitally important and must be kept in mind. As the authors acknowledge, while the connection between this type of behaviour and abusive or neglectful parenting exists, correlation does not equal causation.

Once the theoretical and research background has been established, subsequent chapters describe how different tools can be used in practice and the rationale behind the choices made. Numerous case studies provide solid examples of the positive outcomes emanating from the use of the Pathway Model but, for me, this became rather repetitive. Where I found the most useful information was in the first two chapters and the last four. The descriptions of how the Model was introduced in different London boroughs were enlightening and demonstrate that with the correct structures in place, it can be very effective indeed. The evaluation of the initiative in Enfield, for instance, offers quantitative evidence of success, shows how practitioners fell into three distinct groups depending on their satisfaction with the outcomes, and explains how having other practitioners as mentors significantly increases the use and effectiveness of the Model. Similarly, in Lewisham the researchers found improvements in social work practice and a more satisfied and confident workforce, something that many children's services teams would welcome.

It is clear that the ADAM Project Pathway Model shares some of its genes with developments emanating from the Anna Freud Centre, particularly the application of techniques to encourage explicit mentalisation in parents. In my work with families caring for children who have experienced early trauma, I have found this to pay dividends in improving parenting. What the book offers in addition is a toolbox that can be drawn upon in different situations and in various combinations.

Promoting the Health of Children in Public Care by Florence Merredew and Carolyn Sampeys (eds) London: BAAF (2015) 336 pages. £19.95. ISBN 978 1 910039 26 7

Reviewed by Jean Harris-Hendriks, Retired Senior Lecturer in Child and Adolescent Psychiatry, UK

This book is rich in BAAF tradition and makes me remember with pride my membership of the Medical Group under the chairmanship of Dr Tina Cooper and how much I learned then. The introduction emphasises the former charity's life-enriching contributions to the never-ending necessity to commit multidisciplinary skills to work with children and families who require the protection of a family justice system. It is hoped that these will continue under the auspices of the new CoramBAAF Adoption & Fostering Academy.

A list of contributors, from specialist social work, paediatric medicine and nursing, public health, clinical psychology, learning disability, general practice, law and research and development, makes clear the audience to which this book is heartily recommended. Dental health is discussed in detail. Given that only some 40% of the UK population regularly attend a dentist – with far lower figures likely for children who lack a stable home life, perhaps including abuse and neglect – attention to this area of looked after children's care needs is especially welcome. However, I would have liked to read more on visual and auditory impairment.

I was particularly pleased to see Peter Barnes's and Florence Merredew's chapter on quality assurance and service commissioning, a theme deserving a publication in its own right. After first looking at what health professionals need to know about this area, including the importance of keeping up to date with best practice guidance, the authors explain the roles of individual strategies, such as the Joint Strategic Needs Assessment and the Joint Health and Wellbeing Strategy in England, and how to use these most effectively as essential tools for providing the best possible healthcare services to looked after children.

Other topics include consent and legal provision, health promotion, disabled children, unaccompanied asylum-seeking and other separated children, care leavers and those approaching leaving care, privately fostered children and adult health assessment. Chapter 2 contains some five pages on the health risks for children exposed to alcohol before birth.

The chapters are readily accessible to members of each complementary discipline. There is a section on relevant legislation and the Appendices on current regulations are timely.

An index would be a useful addition to the next edition since this will enable cross-referencing between chapters; for example, I tried to track information about Autism Spectrum Disorders (ASD) across specialisms only with difficulty. I hope that the next edition also will include a contribution from a psychiatrist to complement the very helpful chapter by Geraldine Cresswell, a clinical psychologist writing about the child's mental health and well-being. There will need to be some update about recent developments on the complex interlinks between disorders of attachment and developmental trauma disorder – work that is so helpful to carers and professionals alike.

Currently in the UK, child and adolescent mental health (CAMH) services receive six per cent of the mental health budget yet are expected to serve all young people up to the age of 18 years, as well as to liaise with services for adults; social services departments are trying to continue services to care leavers in addition to all other commitments; the prison service is overcrowded; the needs of asylum-seeking and trafficked children are almost silent; and cuts in legal aid continue. Against this background, there is more need than ever for CoramBAAF as a multidisciplinary forum and agent for research, education and service funding and development. Long may it flourish. This book is a great help.

Abstracts

Adoption & Fostering
2015, Vol. 39(3) 280–283

DOI: 10.1177/0308575915599123
adoptionfostering.sagepub.com

Adoption & Fostering abstracts are selected by Miranda Davies in collaboration with the Social Care Institute for Excellence (SCIE), London. Although care is always taken to be as exact as possible, the editors cannot guarantee the accuracy of material received from outside sources.

Bronell M, Hanlon-Dearman A, Macwilliam L, Chudley A, et al.

Use of health, education and social services by individuals with Fetal Alcohol Spectrum Disorder
Journal of Population Therapeutics and Clinical Pharmacology 20(2), 2013, e95–e106, Canada

FASD is the leading cause of intellectual disability in western society, presenting a significant burden on health, education and social services. Quantifying this burden is important for service planning and policy and programme development. The aim was to describe the health, education and social services use of individuals with FASD to provide an indication of the burden of service use of the disorder. Using a matched cohort design, health, education and social services data were linked with clinical records on individuals 6+ years diagnosed with FASD between 1999/2000 and 2009/10 (n = 717). Matching was 2:1 with a general population and asthma group by age, sex and area-level income. Adjusted rates and relative risks were calculated using Generalized Linear Models. Hospitalisations were higher in the FASD compared to the general population and asthma groups, whereas for physician visits and overall prescriptions, the FASD group differed from only the general population group. Antibiotics, painkillers and anti-psychotics were similar across groups whereas antidepressants and psychostimulants were higher in the FASD group. ADHD was higher in the FASD than the general population and asthma groups. Education and social services use was higher for the FASD than either of the other groups for all measures: receipt of any special education funding; family receipt of income assistance; child in care; and receipt of child welfare services. The findings highlight the need for multisystem supports for those with FASD and comprehensive prevention programmes.

Dumont L

Exploring strategies developed by parents to support their adopted children with foetal alcohol spectrum disorder
Masters dissertation, University of London, Goldsmiths College, 2011, UK

The purpose of this MA dissertation was to discover the strategies developed by adoptive parents to support their children with FASD. The paper begins with a literature review looking at how prenatal exposure to alcohol affects foetal development, and how it manifests in the child and young person's behaviour, cognition, educational achievement, and ability to integrate into society. Nine participants were interviewed for the qualitative phase of the project. Analysis of these interviews revealed that the adoptive parents faced similar struggles in regards to keeping their children safe and obtaining adequate educational provisions. All the participants mentioned the importance of routine, consistency and repetition. They expressed frustration and, at times, anger with professionals (e.g. social care, health and education agencies) when confronted by a lack of awareness and understanding of FASD, as well as disbelief of their experiences and dismissal of their knowledge and expertise as adoptive parents with regard to their children's condition.

Goh YI, Chudley AE, Clarren SK, Koren G, Orrbine E, Rosales T and Rosenbaum C

Task force for development of FASD screening tools: development of Canadian screening tools for Fetal Alcohol Spectrum Disorder
Canadian Journal of Clinical Pharmacology 15(2), 2008, e344–e66, Canada

FASD is the most common cause of neuro-behavioural disability in North America. Screening for it may facilitate diagnosis and hence management of these children. We present a variety of screening tools for the identification of children at risk for FASD. We critically reviewed and evaluated published and practised methods for their potential of screening suspected cases, their epidemiological characteristics (sensitivity, specificity, positive and negative predictive values) [Phase I], as well as their feasibility [Phase II]. The following five tools were selected for the FASD screening toolkit: screening fatty acid ethyl esters in neonatal meconium; the modified Child Behaviour Checklist; Medicine Wheel tool; Asante Centre Probation Officer Tool; and maternal history of drinking and drug use. By screening different populations, from newborns to young people and at-risk mothers, it is anticipated that the toolkit will facilitate diagnosis of FASD.

Gralton E

Foetal alcohol spectrum disorder (FASD): its relevance to forensic adolescent services
Journal of Intellectual Disabilities and Offending Behaviour 5(3), 2014, pp.124–137, UK

There needs to be an increased recognition of FASD in services that deal with young people with disruptive and offending behaviour, not just those services that deal with adolescents with a recognised intellectual disability. This is a general review of the current available evidence on FASD and how it is likely to predispose affected young people to have contact with secure mental health services and the criminal justice system. FASD is likely to have become a more common cause of intellectual disability and behavioural disturbance but the history of significant alcohol exposure in utero is often missed. There is evidence that the hyperactivity is less responsive to psychotropic medication and may represent a different condition to conventional ADHD. However the majority of those affected are in the low normal IQ range. There is so far very limited research into what is likely to be a relatively common disorder with significant costs to criminal justice, mental health care and social services. Epidemiological information from the UK is lacking and urgently needed.

Professionals who work with mentally disordered young people need to be more aware of FASD and its potential contribution to the problems and disabilities in their population. Social workers, foster carers and adoptive parents also need to be more aware of FASD and how it can contribute to the breakdown of social care. There is currently no other review of FASD and the implications for criminal justice, secure mental health and social care for young people.

Marcellus L

Supporting resilience in foster families: a model for program design that supports recruitment, retention, and satisfaction of foster families who care for infants with prenatal substance exposure
Child Welfare Journal 89(1), 2010, pp. 7–29, Canada

The aim of this qualitative research study, conducted in British Columbia, Canada, was to identify the process of becoming a foster family and providing family foster caregiving within the context of caring for infants with prenatal drug and alcohol exposure. The sample consisted of 11 families in five different communities, with data collection through family interviews. The study identified a process for foster families developing expertise in this field, and the article describes three main phases: preparing to foster, living as a foster family, and ending the fostering role. It explores the steps within each phase experienced by foster families, and the application of a resiliency framework to the foster care model to indicate how adaptations to the work and function of relationships within the system may help to strengthen the support of foster families, potentially resulting in improved retention and satisfaction.

Proven S

The language profile of school-aged children with Fetal Alcohol Spectrum Disorder (FASD)
Canadian Journal of Speech Language Pathology and Audiology 37(4), 2014, pp. 268–279, Canada

A population-based study of school age children diagnosed with FASD was conducted to evaluate the language abilities of these children and describe their language strengths and weaknesses. A retrospective chart review methodology was applied to examine their language abilities. Secondary data from 124 children aged 5 to 18 years, who were diagnosed with FASD between January 2005 and October 2010, were included in the study. Results from the CELF-4 language assessment tool were analysed to compare the language abilities of these children. This study revealed globally poor performance across expressive and receptive language abilities, suggesting that language development is significantly affected by prenatal alcohol exposure. The Core Language Index Scores (total test scores) showed almost 70% of the participants received a language rating of 'severe' (indicating significant communication impairments). About 20% had a rating of either 'moderate' or 'mild', and fewer than 15% had a rating of 'average'. Approximately 85% of the sample experienced mild to severe language delays in the index categories. The 5- to 8-year-old age group had the highest average scores in all index categories, whereas the 9-year-olds consistently had the lowest average scores. The changing profile by age group is significant with important ramifications on longitudinal language testing and programming. A better understanding of language abilities in children with prenatal alcohol exposure may lead to improved planning for language interventions.

Wengel T, Hanlon-Dearman A and Fjeldsted B

Sleep and sensory characteristics in young children with FASD
Journal of Developmental Behavioural Pediatrics 32(5), 2011, pp. 384–392, USA

Sleep disruption has been recognised as a clinically important symptom of FASD that has multiple negative effects on the child's health, ability to function adaptively, as well as on family and caregivers. However, few studies have addressed and characterised the sleep problems in this population. The objective of this study was to characterise sleep in FASD and describe the impact of sensory processing difficulties on sleep patterns in children with FASD. Children with FASD were compared with age-matched typically developing children between three and six years of age. Sleep was assessed using actigraphy, a sleep log, and the Children's Sleep Habits Questionnaire. The Sensory Profile™, completed by caregivers, was used to evaluate the child's sensory processing abilities. Overall differences in sensory processing were correlated with actigraphic parameters measured in alcohol exposed and control groups. Data show that children with FASD have significantly more sleep disturbances than typically developing children, including increased bedtime resistance, shortened sleep duration, increased sleep anxiety, and increased night awakenings and parasomnias. Actigraphy reveals a significant difference between groups for sleep onset latency. This study demonstrates that sensory processing deficits are widespread in children with FASD and that these deficits are associated with multiple sleep problems. Children with FASD should be screened for sleep-related disorders and would benefit from occupational therapy for sensory-based treatment aimed at sleep regulation and consolidation.

Whitehurst T

Raising a child with foetal alcohol syndrome: hearing the parent voice
British Journal of Learning Disabilities 40(3), September 2012, pp.187–193, UK

FASD covers a range of conditions, including foetal alcohol syndrome (FAS), which impact upon a child's physical, mental, cognitive and behavioural development. Learning of a child's disability can be a difficult time for any parent. However, parents of children with FASD may have additional difficulties around professional understanding, acknowledgement of the disorder and availability of appropriate support services and structures. The aim of this study was to explore the experiences of both adoptive and birth parents of children with a diagnosis of FAS. Four mothers (3 adoptive and 1 birth) took part in an interview to describe what life was like for them. Six overarching themes emerged from analysis of these stories: first becoming aware that something was wrong; experiencing the disorder as a challenge; experiencing difference; experiencing emotional conflict; experiencing disability; and experiencing support. The findings show that for families to feel supported by professionals, they need to be listened to and their concerns to be heard and acted upon.

coramBAAF
ADOPTION & FOSTERING ACADEMY

ʗoramBAAF Publications

TLES ON HEALTH CARE

Promoting the health of children in public care – The essential guide for health and social work professionals and commissioners

Edited by Florence Merredew and Carolyn Sampeys

With contributions from experienced medical and social work practitioners, this guide provides comprehensive advice on all aspects of the health of looked after and adopted children and their families, along with summaries of the relevant legislation, regulations and guidance. Individual chapters follow a child's journey through care and include information on: the health of looked after children, including mental health and well-being; pathways through care and issues of consent; the particular needs of groups of vulnerable children, including black and minority ethnic children, unaccompanied asylum-seeking children, those who are privately fostered or adopted from overseas, and care leavers; the assessment of adult carers, and common health concerns; confidentiality, information sharing and management of health records; and quality assurance, audit, clinical governance and commissioning.

£19.95 306pp 235x170mm ISBN 978 1 910039 26 7

Donald Forrester

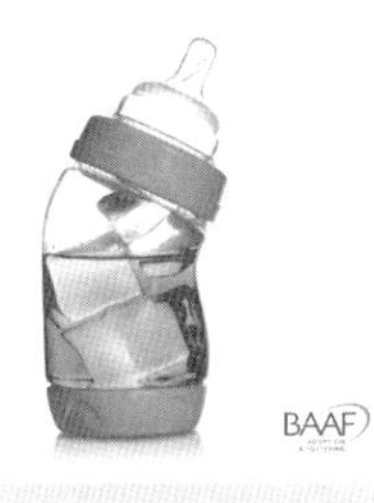

Parenting a child affected by parental substance misuse

Donald Forrester

This handbook provides expert knowledge about parental substance misuse, coupled with facts, figures and guidance presented in a straightforward and accessible style. Adopters and foster carers also describe ıat it is like to parent an affected child, "telling it e it is", sharing their parenting experiences and fering useful advice. It explores general issues ound substance misuse and children entering care well as the impact on children of exposure to bstances during pregnancy, including both specific fects (such as Foetal Alcohol Syndrome) and wider ues (such as genetic susceptibilities).

.95 100pp 198x129mm ISBN 978 1 907585 47 0

Children exposed to parental substance misuse – Implications for family placement

Edited by Rena Phillips

Aimed at both families and professionals, this book tackles practice, policy and research issues. Comprehensive and extensive in scope it explores a wide range of topics including: the role of the medical adviser; the effects of drug (including psychoactive drugs), alcohol and tobacco misuse in pregnancy and beyond; the challenge for social workers when planning for children of substance misusing parents; attachment processes; care planning; the challenges of making placements; therapeutic interventions; and helping the vulnerable child in school. Vividly illustrated with case examples and first person accounts, this collection provides a solid foundation for all those dealing with the consequences of parental substance misuse.

£16.95 328pp 210x147mm ISBN 978 1 903699 27 0

To find out more about these titles, or to place an order, visit www.baaf.org.uk/bookshop or telephone CoramBAAF Publications on 020 7520 7515 or email pubs.sales@baaf.org.uk.

;oramBAAF Publications

IEW EDITION

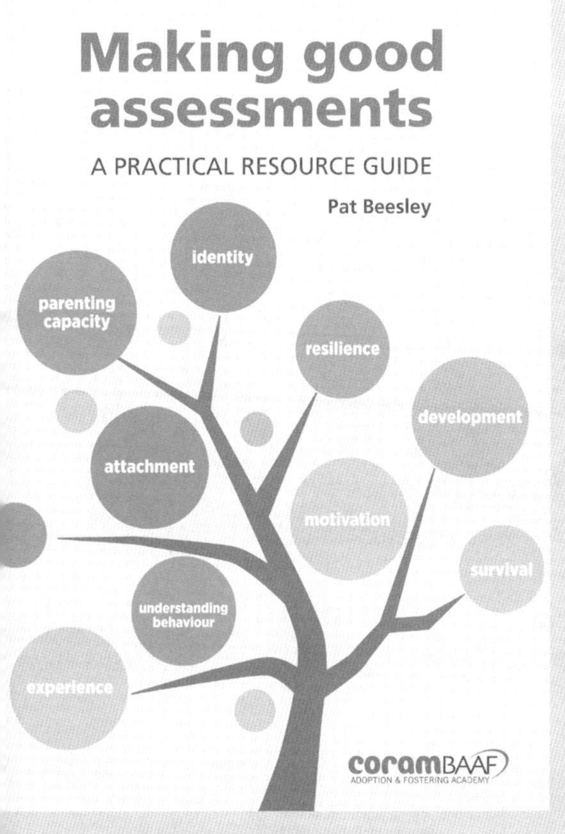

Making good assessments

Pat Beesley

Preparing and assessing potential adopters and permanent foster carers is key to a successful placement. **Making good assessments** is a practical resource guide that is designed to help agencies and family-finding services develop their own assessment programmes. It will help to provide knowledge and understanding to underpin assessments; it can be used flexibly within group settings, individual or family discussion; it fits with current thinking and philosophy but allows scope for development; and provides a broad-based foundation that can be built upon for ongoing work.

The major themes, which are presented as eight modules, will enable an exploration and understanding of:

- attachment, loss and trauma;
- the motivation to parent and expectations of children;
- the impact on the family, resilience and survival;
- parenting capacity;
- identity and difference;
- contact and children's needs;
- the particular needs of children already in the family;
- the issues arising for applicants from different groups, e.g. single, lesbian and gay, and disabled.

ch module provides a broad introduction to the topic, along with articles and excerpts from experts, and esents a range of imaginative exercises to be used with applicants and children. The guide also contains useful se scenarios that can be referred to as well as a comprehensive bibliography.

is authoritative guide will enable family placement workers to approach their assessments with greater nfidence. It will ensure that they address key areas, embrace a holistic approach, and attain high standards. is is an invaluable guide for adoption and fostering workers, panel members, decision makers and those sponsible for making successful placements of children.

:9.95 272pp A4 ISBN 978 1 910039 30 4

To find out more, or to place an order, visit www.corambaaf.org.uk/bookshop or telephone CoramBAAF Publications on 020 7520 7517 or email pubs.sales@corambaaf.org.uk.